SUN QUICK CROSSWORD PUZZLES

ACROSS

7 Occasion to let off fireworks (7,5)

8 Grounds of a university (6)

9 Distasteful, vulgar (5)

10 Throws away (8)

13 Lacking money (4)

15 Greek goats' milk cheese (4)

16 Attendance at an event (8)

17 Root vegetable that is sometimes mashed (5)

19 Failure to win (6)

21 Complete and sincere (12)

DOWN

1 Material such as emery or pumice (8)

2 Children's card game (4)

3 Plane's take-off and landing area (8)

4 Send a message on a mobile phone (4)

5 Follower or believer, such as one of Christ's twelve Apostles (8)

6 Part of milk separated from the curd (4)

11 Daddy-long-legs (8)

12 Motorcycle racing track (8)

14 Gardens where apples or pears may be grown (8)

17 District in central London (4)

18 Bounced sound (4)

20 Destiny (4)

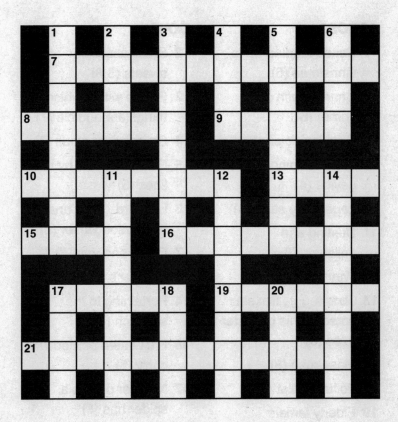

ACROSS

1 Period leading up to Christmas (6)

5 Charge (with a crime) (6)

8 Drinking noisily (8)

9 Car's warning device (4)

10 Legendary story (4)

11 Dusting and polishing (8)

12 Very dirty (6)

13 James ___, film star noted for his gangster roles (6)

15 Mass rush (8)

18 Polluted mist (4)

19 Elderly female relative (4)

20 Ruled (8)

21 One who accompanies another to social functions (6)

22 Summon back or bring to mind (6)

DOWN

2 Small assorted sweets (5,8)

3 Range within which things are audible (7)

4 On edge, nervous (7)

5 Corner formed by two lines (5)

6 Leonard ___, Canadian singer/songwriter (5)

7 Oddly enough (7,2,4)

13 Butcher's chopper (7)

14 Pertaining to the stomach (7)

16 Fruit eaten pickled with curry (5)

17 Number of legs a spider has (5)

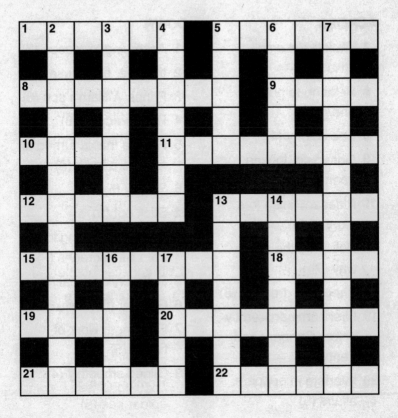

ACROSS

7 Walk like a small child (6)

8 Relating to nuclear energy (6)

9 Bee colony (4)

10 Observed, looked upon (8)

11 Pleasant finish to a story (5,6)

14 Returned the same way (7,4)

18 Shocking, dreadful (8)

19 First name shared by actors Connery and Penn (4)

20 Interfere in people's affairs (6)

21 Departed (6)

DOWN

1 According to reason (7)

2 Inactive, out of use (4)

3 Prince William's son (6)

4 Rough-edged (6)

5 Handle that is turned to release a latch (8)

6 Sleepy (5)

12 Stick out (8)

13 Tool for removing ice from windscreens (7)

15 Self-service meal (6)

16 Go over (the limit) (6)

17 Full-length work of fiction (5)

19 Glided smoothly (4)

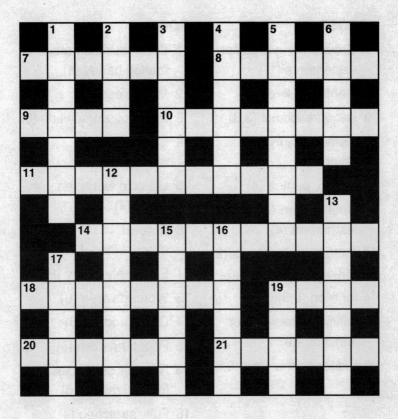

ACROSS

7 Groups living together, settlements (11)

8 Gentle walk (6)

9 Become extinct (3,3)

10 Name (a baby) in church (8)

11 Puffed, panted (4)

12 Double-reed orchestral instrument (4)

14 Picture explanations (8)

17 Formal neckwear item for men (3,3)

19 Official agreement or sanction (6)

20 Indoor sports area (6,5)

DOWN

1 Drink distilled from malted barley (6)

2 Motionless (8)

3 Piece of ammunition (6)

4 Concealed, obscured (6)

5 US coin worth ten cents (4)

6 Shrewd, sharp-witted (6)

11 Extremely happy (8)

13 Woman's shirt (6)

14 Dairy product (6)

15 Popular flatfish (6)

16 Number of minutes in a football match (6)

18 Fully stretched (4)

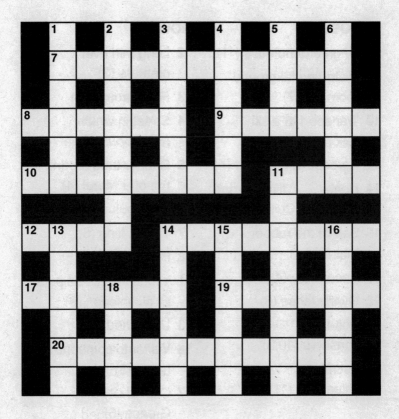

ACROSS

1 Degree of hotness (11)
9 Distorting fairground room (4,2,7)
10 Transport at a ski resort (5-3)
12 Agreeable, pleasant (4)
14 *Home* ___, film starring Macaulay Culkin (5)
15 Sap of the rubber tree (5)
19 Encourage (4)
20 Overly tense (8)
22 Soft-fruit conserve (10,3)
24 Estimates, valuations (11)

DOWN

2 Long thin river creature (3)
3 Food groups (8)
4 Street in which *Neighbours* is set (6)
5 Rubber tube around the rim of a wheel (4)
6 Spacious quality (9)
7 Throw, fling (5)
8 Burnt remains (5)
11 Young female helpers at Wimbledon (9)
13 Unworried (8)
16 Visitor to someone's home (5)
17 Capital city of Greece (6)
18 Bryan ___, pop singer (5)
21 Quaint, cute (4)
23 Stick (out) (3)

ACROSS

1 Terror-stricken (6,5)
9 Cash dispenser (inits) (3)
10 Stretch too far (9)
11 *Here We Go round the ___ Bush*, children's song (8)
12 King of the jungle (4)
14 Creamed (potatoes) (6)
16 Symptom of a cold (6)
18 Red stone (4)
19 Attractive personal allure (8)
22 Makes familiar with (9)
23 Ancient (3)
24 Poisonous viper which makes a noise by shaking its tail (11)

DOWN

2 Desert animal (5)
3 Started trading again (shop) (8)
4 Cheerless, gloomy (6)
5 Become weary (4)
6 Easily breakable (7)
7 Monument honouring dead soldiers (3,8)
8 Pass to a different owner (6,5)
13 Jailed (2,6)
15 Underwater swimming (3-4)
17 Fortune or opportunity (6)
20 Appal, horrify (5)
21 Seasoning on crisps (4)

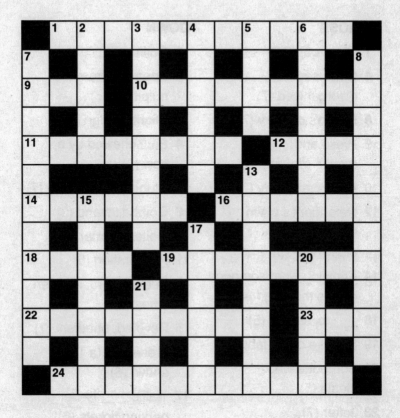

ACROSS

1 Clear off! (3,2)

4 Confused, disorganised (7)

8 Dublin's country (7)

9 Press and stretch (dough) (5)

10 Aristocratic lady (7)

12 Defendant's claim of having been elsewhere (5)

14 Knowing what someone else is thinking (4-7)

18 ___ to, should (5)

19 Silk-like dress fabric (7)

21 Someone who steals (5)

23 Jotter (7)

24 Progress, advance (7)

25 Long-legged wading bird (5)

DOWN

1 Coiffure (6)

2 Speaking from the pulpit (9)

3 Slightest sign (5)

4 Stuff chewed by a cow (3)

5 Stubborn or clumsy (7)

6 Golf-ball stand (3)

7 Golfer's porter (6)

11 Perspiration (5)

13 Pub landlord, in olden times (9)

15 Devoted, obedient (7)

16 Presented (a TV show) (6)

17 Traffic ___, issuer of parking tickets (6)

20 Go and get (5)

22 UK commercial broadcasting company (inits)(3)

23 Short sleep (3)

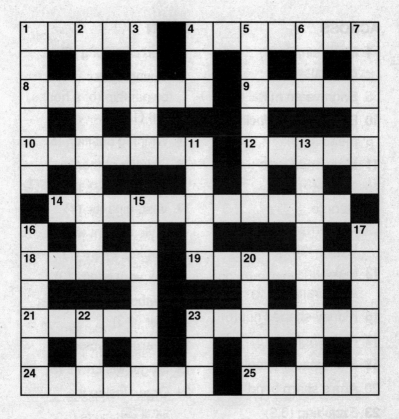

ACROSS

1 Make simpler to understand (7)

5 Engrave on metal (4)

10 Black road-surfacing material (3)

11 Mum and Dad's duties (9)

12 George ___, mastermind of the *Star Wars* saga (5)

13 Make an appearance (4,2)

15 Kidney-shaped nut (6)

17 Pig's shrill cry (6)

18 Stonemason's tool (6)

20 Arm's sharp bend (5)

23 Excluding (6,3)

24 Up in the ___, still undecided (3)

25 ___ up, feel more cheerful (4)

26 Altering (7)

DOWN

2 Part of a song (5)

3 Taking back ownership (of a house, eg) (12)

4 Winning position (5)

6 Speech of thanks, expression of praise (7)

7 Vast, gigantic (4)

8 Style of print with sloping letters (7)

9 Not very often (12)

14 Method of styling wet hair (4-3)

16 Learned person (7)

19 Singer Ms Lewis (5)

21 Organ inside the skull (5)

22 Let fall to the ground (4)

ACROSS

1 Food preparation instruction list (6)

4 Put the phone down (4,2)

9 Private transport (3)

10 County town in the Midlands (9)

11 Nearly vertical (cliff face) (5)

12 Undo (knitting) (7)

14 Constant, perpetual (5-6)

17 Variety show at a restaurant (7)

18 1979 Sigourney Weaver sci-fi film (5)

20 Grilled over charcoal (9)

22 Muhammad ___, famous boxer (3)

23 Housetop worker (6)

24 Stick fast (6)

DOWN

1 Alcove, niche (6)

2 Evil spell (5)

3 Arctic animal (5,4)

5 Beer (3)

6 Punish someone who did something to you (3,4)

7 Danger (5)

8 Find an answer (6,2,3)

13 (Caught) in the act of wrongdoing (3-6)

15 Government trade ban (7)

16 Ask (to a party) (6)

17 Pole tossed or hurled by Highland athletes (5)

19 Extremely angry (5)

21 Woolly farm female (3)

ACROSS

8 Science of the body's structure (7)

9 Second meal of the day, usually (5)

10 Red-nosed joker (5)

11 Brown plant washed up on the beach (7)

12 Keep up with other runners (5,3,4)

16 Focusing on one aim (6-6)

20 Nourish and rear (7)

23 Makes corrections to (text) (5)

24 Melodious sounds (5)

25 Moping (7)

DOWN

1 Sports fixture (5)

2 Denise ___, actress and TV presenter (3,5)

3 Take part, lend a hand (4,2)

4 Seed-buds in potatoes (4)

5 Sordid political goings-on (6)

6 First name of US actress Ms Hathaway (4)

7 Shiver with horror (7)

13 ___ Cruise, *Mission: Impossible* star (3)

14 Pre-dinner drink (8)

15 Frightening tidal wave (7)

17 Official release of a new product (6)

18 Knitting tool (6)

19 Habitual practice (5)

21 Danger (4)

22 Make less painful (4)

ACROSS

7 Bird with a large brightly coloured tail (7)

9 Item from the past (5)

10 Childminder (5)

11 Soft running shoe (7)

12 ___ Vegas, American city famous for its casinos (3)

13 Undoing, ruination (8)

16 On the father's side (8)

17 Female parent (3)

19 Porridge ingredient (7)

21 ___ Jackson, female singer (5)

22 Joint linking the foot and leg (5)

23 High swing for acrobats (7)

DOWN

1 Long thin (legs) (7)

2 Milk of ___, stomach medicine (8)

3 Hunky ___, all OK (4)

4 Terrible, shocking (8)

5 ___ Carr, stand-up comedian (4)

6 Terrifying (5)

8 Actress who starred in *Iris* and *Titanic* (4,7)

13 Became more profound (8)

14 Spoke mournfully of (8)

15 Suffocate (7)

18 Whole (5)

20 Consume (medicine) (4)

21 ___ of Arc, famous martyr (4)

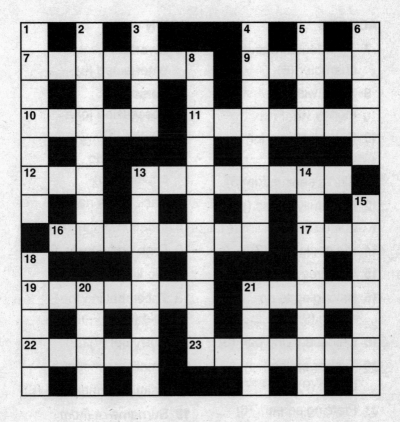

ACROSS

7 ___ Mouse, Disney character (6)

8 Trade without money (6)

10 Carved shape for display (9)

11 Skirt's sewn edge (3)

12 Forcefully stress (a point) (5,4)

14 Pig enclosure (3)

15 Evergreen tree (3)

16 Belonging to no nation (9)

18 Chinese frying pan (3)

20 Timber on the beach (9)

21 Piercing scream (6)

22 Person who paints or draws (6)

DOWN

1 Diverted, entertained (6)

2 Person in possession (of a house) (8)

3 Unable to do anything (8)

4 Back of the neck (4)

5 Irritation of the skin (4)

6 Drab and dowdy (6)

9 Working by itself (9)

13 Those having the vote (8)

14 Hurry up! (4,2,2)

15 Smallest amount (6)

17 Calm and unhurried (6)

19 Surname of *From Here to Eternity* star Deborah (4)

20 Fight over a matter of honour (4)

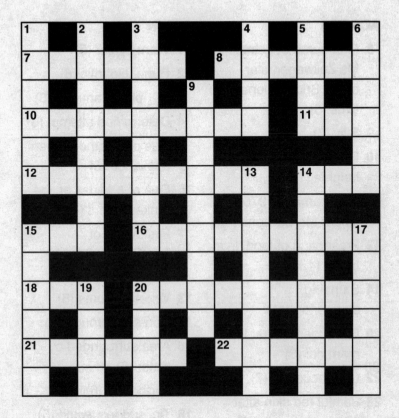

ACROSS

8 First name of actress Ms Zellweger, star of the Bridget Jones films (5)

9 Silly (7)

10 Dizziness from heights (7)

11 First name of 1970s singer Ms Carpenter (5)

12 Preserving of food, in a fridge (4,7)

14 Stunning, staggering (11)

20 Endangered bear-like mammal (5)

22 Car document (7)

23 Painful red skin after too much tanning (7)

24 Communicate via the internet (5)

DOWN

1 Went by car (5)

2 Huge, gigantic (8)

3 ___ piece, antique (6)

4 Determined attempt (6)

5 Gas or electric kitchen appliance (6)

6 One of a series of ranked layers (4)

7 First name of *EastEnders* actor Mr Richie (5)

13 Venetian boats (8)

15 Non-see-through (6)

16 Area surrounded by water (6)

17 Further up (6)

18 Tic, sudden twitch (5)

19 Head's bony framework (5)

21 Number of skittle pins (4)

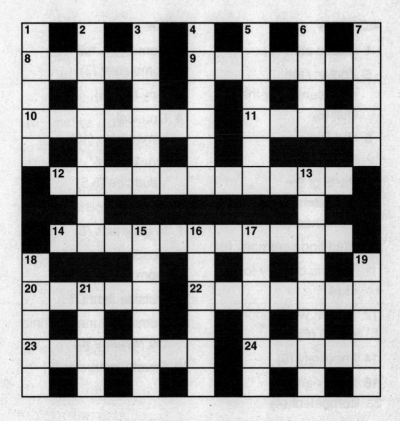

ACROSS

1 Chase after (6)

5 Zodiac sign, represented by the Bull (6)

8 Old Russian emperor (4)

9 Parts of the feet, sometimes varnished (8)

10 Wedding ceremony (8)

11 ___ on, be very fond of (4)

12 Person who performs on ice (6)

14 Impolitely (6)

16 Clever and competent (4)

18 Goading, provoking (8)

20 Outer motorway section (4,4)

21 Of rain, fall heavily (4)

22 Pretty, charming (6)

23 Queen's chair (6)

DOWN

2 Come ___, fail completely (7)

3 Tiny fish (5)

4 Unusual, remarkable (13)

5 Trunk full of valuables (8,5)

6 Without assistance (7)

7 In darkness (5)

13 Hospital operating room (7)

15 Outside light (7)

17 Comic featuring Dennis the Menace (5)

19 Private instructor (5)

ACROSS

1 Slightly intoxicated (5)
4 Govern harshly and keep in subservience (7)
9 System that can be surfed (8)
10 Ooze, trickle (4)
11 Santa's cave (6)
12 Rented (a car, eg) (5)
13 Image not in focus (4)
15 Fixed bench in a church (3)
16 Uncommon (4)
17 Country's set of ships (5)
19 Trainee nun (6)
21 Measure of medicine (4)
22 Hypersensitive, obsessive (8)
23 Person holding a commission in the army (7)
24 Eating and drinking spree (5)

DOWN

2 Opposite of 'outer' (5)
3 Bus-stop structure (7)
5 Alarm, frighten (3,3,4,2)
6 Upright part of a staircase between treads (5)
7 Thin in an attractive way (7)
8 Lack of ability (12)
14 Commence rocket flight (4,3)
16 Italian dish of meat in pasta 'cushions' (7)
18 ___ Sandé, singer (5)
20 Hold on tightly (5)

ACROSS

1 Very best, most favourable (7)

5 Rapid economic collapse (5)

9 Person or thing well known to the public (9,4)

10 Edited to remove offensive material (8)

11 Punch and Judy's dog (4)

12 Item of table linen (9)

16 Body part with a heel and arch (4)

17 Had a chinwag (8)

19 To a certain extent (5,1,7)

21 Garment worn on the top half (5)

22 Milk from which the cream has been removed (7)

DOWN

2 Insincere person (6)

3 Determined, forceful (9)

4 Official escorting people to seats (5)

6 Dispute (3)

7 High-intensity flashing beam of light (6)

8 Fun vehicle for the snow (6)

11 ___ Hotspur, north London soccer club (9)

13 Person who destroys or spoils things (6)

14 Hard bath sponge (6)

15 Crack (a hidden message) (6)

18 Express gratitude to (5)

20 Make mistakes (3)

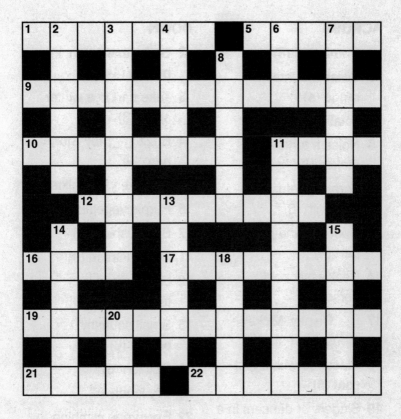

S^{THE}un

ACROSS

1 Comforted (8)

6 Swiss mountain range (4)

8 Totalling up (6)

9 Noise a turkey makes (6)

10 Formally refuses to deal with (8)

13 Underground plant part (4)

14 Recklessly bold person (9)

17 ___ Disney, Mickey Mouse's creator (4)

18 Plastered with a first coat (8)

19 Singers or dancers in a show (6)

21 Sultana-like dried fruit (6)

23 Knob on the sole of a football boot (4)

24 Having little money (5,3)

DOWN

2 Better than even, in betting (4-2)

3 Take part in a winter sport (3)

4 Buzz ___, *Toy Story* hero (9)

5 Pet taken for walkies (3)

6 Purple vegetable (9)

7 Bed cushion (6)

11 Hired, leased (9)

12 Losing your temper (6,3)

15 Small squashy packet (6)

16 Opinion (6)

20 Cry loudly (3)

22 Evergreen climbing plant (3)

ACROSS

1 Refuse to admit (4)
4 Doctor's clients (8)
8 Most uncommon (6)
9 Non-commissioned sailor (6)
10 Care for, look after (4)
11 ___ for, desiring strongly (8)
13 Brass instrument (5,8)
16 Altering to suit (8)
19 Meat-substitute bean (4)
20 Caution with money (6)
22 Great South American river (6)
23 Adds sugar to (8)
24 Building plot (4)

DOWN

2 Given a hard coating (9)
3 Accepted defeat (7)
4 Toddler's toilet (5)
5 Violent whirlwind (7)
6 (Had) consumed (5)
7 Light brown colour (3)
12 Mother of a kid (5-4)
14 Prickly Scottish emblem (7)
15 Travel voucher given to senior citizens or disabled people (3,4)
17 Force (open) (5)
18 Lawn plant (5)
21 In what way? (3)

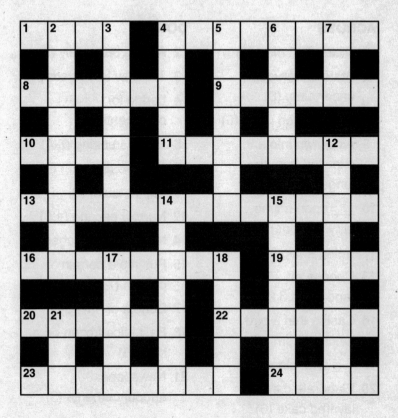

ACROSS

1 Bible's first man (4)
4 State of nervous uncertainty (8)
8 Dirty blurred mark (6)
9 Air drawn into and expelled from the lungs (6)
10 ___ upon a time, fairy-tale opening (4)
11 Being anxious (8)
13 Choose at random (4,3,2,1,3)
16 Casing that a bird hatches from (8)
19 ___ Ora, singer (4)
20 Elaborate creamy layered cake (6)
22 Green, yellow or red pulse (6)
23 Handily (8)
24 Highly strung, twitchy (4)

DOWN

2 Asking brusquely (9)
3 Tuesday to Thursday (7)
4 Ledge for ornaments (5)
5 Below freezing (3-4)
6 Choose (by vote) (5)
7 Lay (a table) (3)
12 Narrow escape (4,5)
14 Not evenly matched (7)
15 Put into a certain pattern (7)
17 Bundle of hay (5)
18 Fruit juice frozen on a stick (5)
21 Newspaper announcements (3)

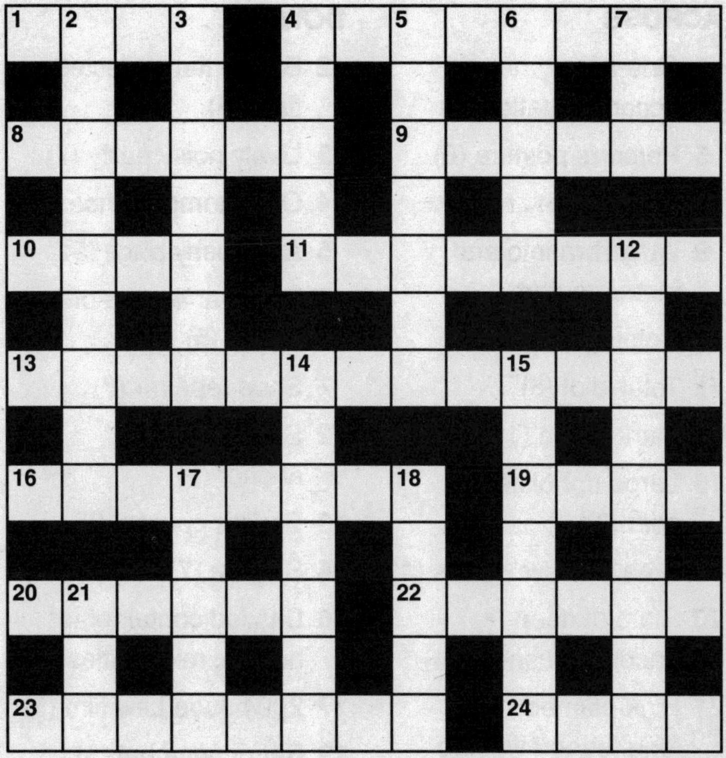

ACROSS

1 One-room accommodation (6)

5 Person's posture (6)

8 Smarter (8)

9 Large brass-band instrument (4)

10 Coloured (hair) (4)

11 Total idiot (8)

12 Marker pen (11)

15 Large upholstered seat (8)

18 Area of mown grass (4)

20 State of deep unconsciousness (4)

21 Pink-plumed, long-legged wading bird (8)

22 Country of which Athens is the capital (6)

23 Fruity dessert in a pot (6)

DOWN

2 Before the expected time (5)

3 Lively noisy party (7)

4 Of little importance (7)

5 Any bushy plant (5)

6 Room at the top of a house (5)

7 Shoe repairer (7)

12 Ship's place to anchor (7)

13 Berlin's country (7)

14 Sloping (7)

16 Divided container for holding milk bottles (5)

17 2004 Jude Law film (5)

19 Bet or lay a bet (5)

ACROSS

7 Coincide partially (7)

9 Exciting, intoxicating (5)

10 ___ Brown, author of the thriller *The Da Vinci Code* (3)

11 Special knowledge (9)

12 Layer of the atmosphere said to be damaged by pollution (5)

14 Monarch's family (7)

16 Child's word for a confectionery item (7)

18 Unhealthily overweight (5)

19 Lamp at the back of a vehicle (4,5)

20 Useless, worn out (3)

21 Blockade (5)

22 Give as part-payment (5,2)

DOWN

1 Selfish drivers (4,4)

2 Stop giving (a baby) mother's milk (4)

3 Accuse without proof (6)

4 Small fruit with a stone (6)

5 ___ Steel, best-selling author (8)

6 Extravagant publicity (4)

8 Small heavy object used to keep documents in place (11)

13 Performs surgery (8)

15 Giving way (to) (8)

17 Slanted (6)

18 Wild West bandit (6)

19 Pink-coloured (4)

20 Legal document (4)

ACROSS

7 Sharp pains in the side after running (8)

8 Standard or customary behaviour (4)

9 Article, thing (6)

10 Having nothing inside (5)

11 Film spool (4)

12 Acting against (8)

14 Parts of a serial, broadcast separately (8)

18 Tube along which liquid or gas is conveyed (4)

20 Cowboy's rope (5)

22 Shoe liner (6)

23 Call by phone (4)

24 Arouses, elicits (8)

DOWN

1 Farm building for horses (6)

2 Church towers and spires (8)

3 Deprived inner-city area (6)

4 In the Land of Nod (6)

5 Small cut (4)

6 Coloured pencil (6)

13 Fairground booth (8)

15 Preaching platform (6)

16 Floppy, limp (6)

17 Member of the Navy (6)

19 Wayne Rooney's wife (6)

21 Write your name (4)

ACROSS

7 Inundating with water (8)

8 Anger, annoy (4)

9 Hate (6)

10 Queen's youngest son (6)

11 ___ Tracy, Hollywood great (7)

13 Kettle's pouring part (5)

15 Bottom of a room (5)

17 In the direction of, approaching (7)

19 Protective and ornamental covering for a car wheel (3-3)

21 Jumbled mix (6)

23 Light-sabre-wielding knight of the *Star Wars* films (4)

24 Ocean between Britain and America (8)

DOWN

1 Or ___, otherwise (4)

2 Enter a room from outside (4,2)

3 Walked on the balls of the feet (7)

4 Leer at (4)

5 Become an adult (4,2)

6 From every side (3-5)

12 Contaminates, taints (8)

14 Mathematical expression (7)

16 Exotic flower (6)

18 Helping (6)

20 Enjoy a game (4)

22 Revise text (4)

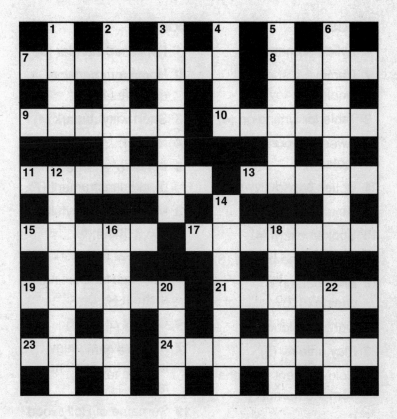

ACROSS

6 Kylie's surname (7)

7 Remove a sheep's wool (5)

9 Table for writing on (4)

10 Sweet-flavoured roots (8)

11 British capital city (6)

13 Defeat (4)

15 Spoken exam (4)

16 Smooth and buttery (6)

18 Blind person's canine (5,3)

21 Light in colour (4)

22 Play unfairly (5)

23 Hold different opinions from the norm (7)

DOWN

1 Published slander (5)

2 Home for shoreline creatures (4,4)

3 Short witty remark (4)

4 Next (4)

5 Player of a large plucked instrument (7)

8 Move about playfully, like a horse (6)

12 Ten-year time period (6)

13 Tall mast for illuminating a street (4-4)

14 Current of air (7)

17 Alternative strategy in case the first one fails (4,1)

19 Surname of Hollywood actress Cameron (4)

20 Severe, stern (4)

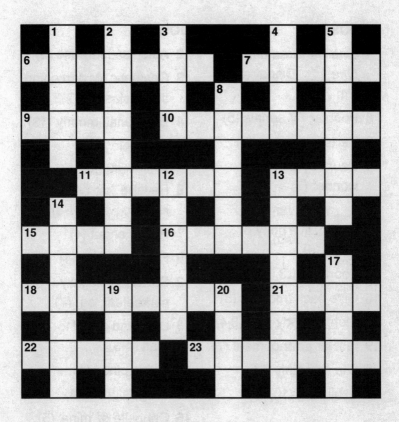

ACROSS

1 *One Hundred and One* ___, Disney's dog film (10)
8 Popular TV serials (5)
9 Ballistic weapon (7)
10 Daunt by arousing wonder (7)
11 ___ wave, large destructive body of water (5)
12 Poorly (2,1,3,3)
15 Give back (money) (5)
17 Pierced body part (3,4)
19 Flower arrangement (7)
20 Slip smoothly (5)
21 Exhibiting (10)

DOWN

2 Astonish, surprise (5)
3 Cosmetic for darkening the eyelashes (7)
4 Emotional, moody (13)
5 Profitable possession (5)
6 Revolve (clothes) to remove water (4-3)
7 Holler, shout (4)
8 Footwear item (4)
12 Seize (an illegally parked car, eg) (7)
13 Lazy and afraid to graft (4-3)
14 In this place (4)
15 Judge's gown (4)
16 Opposite of 'mine' (5)
18 Bulb-like vegetable (5)

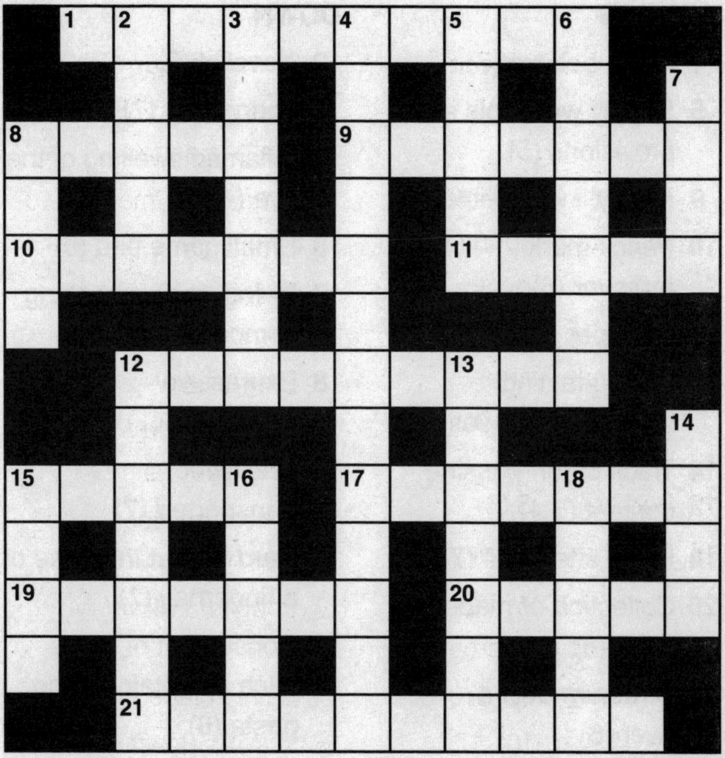
1
2
3
4
5
6
7
8
9
10
11
12
13
14
15
16
17
18
19
20
21

ACROSS

1 Make-believe (7)
5 Supply with tools and provisions (5)
9 Heavy, indigestible (6)
10 Pencil-mark remover (6)
11 Chopper blade (5)
12 Strong-tasting blue-veined cheese (7)
14 Track baton-passing contest (5,4)
18 Flight attendant (7)
20 Collection of maps in a book (5)
22 Structure over a river (6)
23 Fired from a job (6)
24 Bracelet ornament (5)
25 Procession in costume (7)

DOWN

2 Novelist (6)
3 Young frog (7)
4 Inflamed swelling of the eye (4)
6 Small game bird (5)
7 Refrigerator's freezing compartment (6)
8 Expressive movement (7)
13 Conveyed, transported (7)
15 Hard skin at the base of a fingernail (7)
16 Constituent of foods such as potatoes and pasta (6)
17 Old pub (6)
19 Broader (5)
21 India's continent (4)

ACROSS

1 Cow's milk bag (5)

4 Pig food (5)

9 Christian festival often in April (6)

10 Plant cultivated for its blooms (6)

12 Create an advantage out of (4,2,7)

13 Speak for another to write down (7)

18 Truckers' eatery (9,4)

19 ___ O'Leary, TV presenter (6)

20 Take small bites, like a mouse (6)

21 Guy, chap (5)

22 Human ___, person (5)

DOWN

2 Dry wasteland (6)

3 Accident caused by touching bare wires (8,5)

5 Unofficial industrial action (7,6)

6 Legal (6)

7 Fixed bunk on a ship (5)

8 Used a pen (5)

11 Surname of Hollywood star Gwyneth (7)

14 Pore over books (5)

15 Vat, keg (6)

16 ___ footprint, measure of greenhouse gas emissions (6)

17 Precious gem (5)

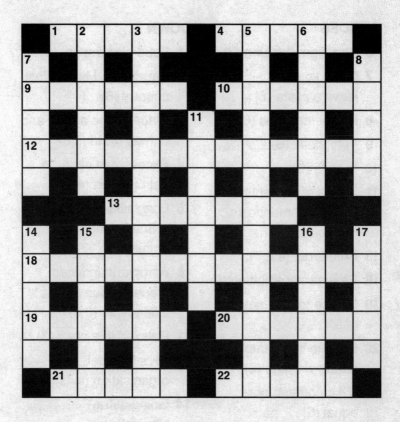

ACROSS

3 Star sign, the Lion (3)

7 Make yourself ___, leave a place (6)

8 Highly regarded (6)

9 Very weak (6)

10 In truth (6)

11 Series of attempts to blacken someone's name (5,8)

13 Shred, cut (4,2,7)

18 Emergency situation (6)

19 Refuse to take notice of (6)

20 Confine in a camp during wartime (6)

21 (Of a contest) not equal (6)

22 Fuel used for cooking and heating (3)

DOWN

1 Loud piercing cry (6)

2 Saudi ___, Middle East country (6)

3 Place where a road and railway meet (5,8)

4 Excessively eager to get on in life (4-9)

5 Long silky wool from a South American animal (6)

6 Aeroplane-induced tiredness due to time differences (3,3)

11 Relaxed in a chair (3)

12 UK's medical organisation (inits)(3)

14 Going astray, sinning (6)

15 Slice of bacon (6)

16 Dealer in a board-game (6)

17 Looked after, cared for (a patient) (6)

ACROSS

5 Having an all-round view (9)

8 Chauvinistic regarding gender (6)

9 Either of two small organs in the throat (6)

10 Toilet (3)

11 Football player permitted to handle the ball (6)

13 Steal in a small way (6)

15 Political refuge (6)

18 Harm, hurt (6)

20 ___ up, admit (3)

21 Reply (6)

22 Visitor, guest (6)

23 Major Hollywood actor or actress (5,4)

DOWN

1 Beauty-salon treatment (6)

2 Plastic or glass container with a neck (6)

3 Portable computer (6)

4 Transmit information by means of a gesture (6)

6 Moving to another home (9)

7 Fruity colour? (4,5)

12 Written promise to pay (inits)(3)

14 Tavern (3)

16 Nigella ___, food writer (6)

17 Gloomy, gruesome (6)

18 Lest, on the off-chance (2,4)

19 ___ Clary, comedian, panellist and TV host (6)

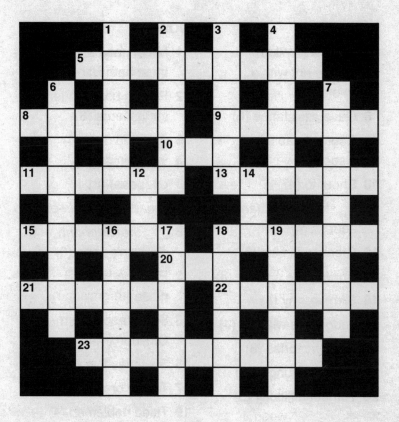

ACROSS

7 Make a forward movement with a sword (6)

8 Gave assistance (6)

9 Country, capital Lisbon (8)

10 Shout to (4)

11 ___ Moore, *GI Jane* actress (4)

12 Creases in skin (8)

14 Hurting like a nettle (8)

16 Slim, skinny (4)

18 Ledge of a window (4)

20 Great victories (8)

22 Die from hunger (6)

23 Without difficulty (6)

DOWN

1 Metal used to plate most bath fittings (6)

2 Person born in Vienna, for instance (8)

3 Antlered deer (4)

4 Taking the pods off (peas) (8)

5 Smart ___, know-all (4)

6 ___ *the Elephant*, children's song (6)

12 Produced a shrill noise (8)

13 Supermodel from Croydon (4,4)

15 Six times five (6)

17 Take a breath (6)

19 Titled nobleman (4)

21 One thing (4)

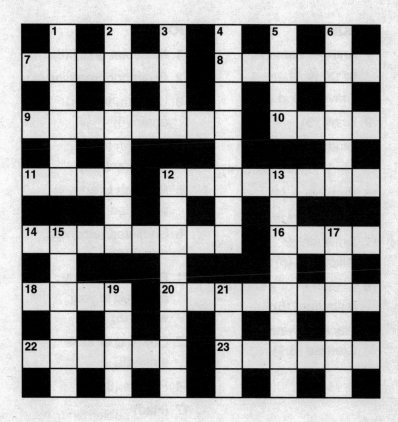

ACROSS

7 Another name for bingo (6-6)

8 Craving food (6)

9 Brawl (5)

10 Hidden dangers (8)

13 Black playing-card (4)

15 Burn black (4)

16 Squeaky clean (8)

17 Drawbacks, difficulties (5)

19 Customer of a shop or restaurant (6)

21 Place for water exercise (8,4)

DOWN

1 Macabre, grisly (8)

2 Organ for breathing (4)

3 Uses (materials) again (8)

4 Cook (in a restaurant) (4)

5 Relating to an operation (8)

6 Undiluted (alcoholic drink) (4)

11 Parts of the body attached to your wrists (8)

12 Downing of tools, strike (8)

14 Pristine (8)

17 (Had) planted (seeds) (4)

18 ___ LaBeouf, US actor (4)

20 Pace of a horse (4)

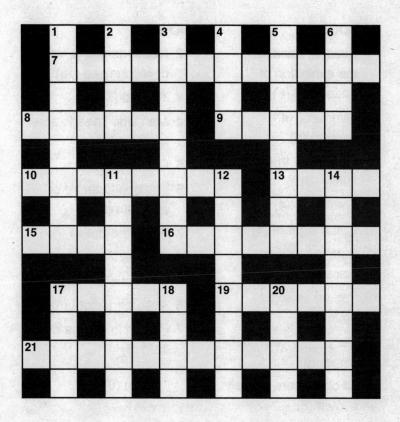

ACROSS

1 Building used for the exhibition of antiquities (6)

5 Overrun (with vermin) (6)

8 Flowers of the daffodil family (8)

9 French fry (4)

10 Catch sight of (4)

11 Aids to block out noise (8)

12 Person selling a house (6)

13 Gary ___, Take That singer (6)

15 Of containers, closely sealed (8)

18 Wicked giant (4)

19 Pack neatly away (4)

20 Process of becoming another's legal parent (8)

21 Muddled, confused (6)

22 Caress, pet (an animal) (6)

DOWN

2 Not understood, valued or recognised (13)

3 Thrilled (7)

4 Man who kneads sore muscles (7)

5 Chillier (5)

6 ___ point, centre of attention (5)

7 Go away (5,4,4)

13 Clothes fasteners (7)

14 Domestic cockerel (7)

16 Absorbent cloth (5)

17 Person in charge of a train (5)

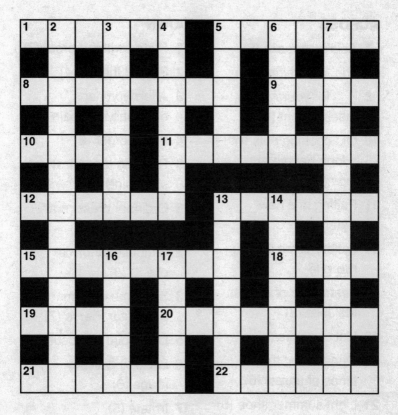

ACROSS

7 Acid's opposite (6)

8 Trip, excursion (3,3)

9 ___ for yourself, be independent (4)

10 Old cooking pots with a long handle and legs (8)

11 Putting in a new order (11)

14 Lottery ticket that you rub (11)

18 First name of actress Ms Jolie (8)

19 List of actors (4)

20 Opportunist thief in times of unrest (6)

21 Light summer shoe (6)

DOWN

1 Stated without proof (7)

2 Settled the bill (4)

3 Afternoon nap, especially in Spain (6)

4 Frilly border (6)

5 Relating to tropical storms (8)

6 Ordinary dress, not uniform (5)

12 Simulate (a former event) (8)

13 Surname of former Bond star Pierce (7)

15 Large bird enclosure (6)

16 Lacking delicacy, rough (6)

17 Irritate (5)

19 Wafer for holding ice cream (4)

ACROSS

7 Proposals or hints (11)

8 Female parent (6)

9 Deadly, fatal (6)

10 Gave a prize to (8)

11 Produced offspring (4)

12 Invites (to a party) (4)

14 Went up like a spacecraft (8)

17 Ceremonial act (6)

19 Parentless child (6)

20 Coin worth one fifth of a pound (6,5)

DOWN

1 On dry land (6)

2 Brainboxes, boffins (8)

3 Dreaded, was worried about (6)

4 Arranged (hair) (6)

5 Verse writer (4)

6 Long-bodied car (6)

11 Contacting by pager (8)

13 Devious-looking (6)

14 Narrate, give an account of (6)

15 Fairly rough (of the sea) (6)

16 Surface coating of teeth (6)

18 One who consumes goods (4)

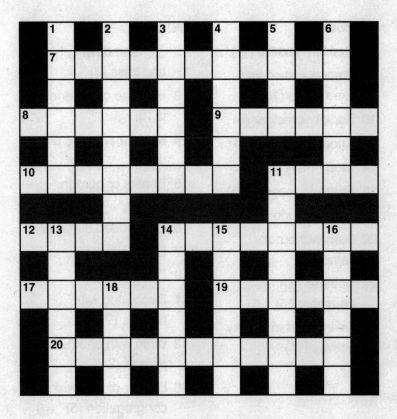

configuration (2)

14 Piece of a performance (9)

16 thousand and ___

specific (6)

21 ___ Rio, the Christmas

display (9)

23 Spirit (5)

ACROSS

1 Garden gazebo (11)

9 Preoccupation with fixed ideas (13)

10 Society-changer (8)

12 Knock senseless (4)

14 Stop briefly (5)

15 Shared (account) (5)

19 Pain (in a tooth) (4)

20 Burn without a flame (8)

22 Knee-length trousers (7,6)

24 Taking part in a risky activity (11)

DOWN

2 ___ and downs, highs and lows (3)

3 Have no confidence in (8)

4 Made a surprise attack on (6)

5 Beasts of burden, cattle (4)

6 With added sugar (9)

7 Excuse me! (5)

8 Consuming (5)

11 Decorated with plumes (9)

13 Write with another person (2-6)

16 Leader of a Jewish congregation (5)

17 Force of a collision (6)

18 Mustard and ___, seedlings (5)

21 ___ log, Christmas dessert (4)

23 Sprint (3)

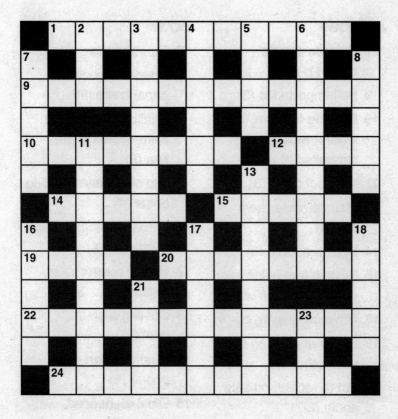

ACROSS

1 Devices that do sums (11)

9 Self-importance (3)

10 Building from which trains are controlled (6,3)

11 Very hot curry (8)

12 Make a noise like a lion (4)

14 Hole in a tooth (6)

16 System that helps drivers find their way (6)

18 Minim or quaver, eg (4)

19 Game of jumping over each other (8)

22 Put (a record) on sale again (2-7)

23 Bright object in the sky (3)

24 Items needed when following a cookbook (11)

DOWN

2 Oak tree seed (5)

3 Hospital's accident department (8)

4 Shallow body of salt water linked to the sea (6)

5 Top of a baby's feeding bottle (4)

6 Prepare (a surface) for painting (3,4)

7 Hub of control for an organisation (5,6)

8 Costing a great deal (11)

13 Listening part of a phone (8)

15 Old experienced person (7)

17 Name that links actors Butler and Depardieu (6)

20 Adjust (an alarm) (5)

21 Speak unclearly, as if drunk (4)

ACROSS

1 Find the answer to (5)
4 Sale where bids are made (7)
8 Comprehensively, thoroughly (2,5)
9 Posed a question (5)
10 Large shellfish (7)
12 Crime of stealing (5)
14 Novelist subject of a 2001 film starring Kate Winslet and Judi Dench (4,7)
18 Magazine edition (5)
19 During the course of a journey (2,5)
21 Jewelled head-dress (5)
23 Distant planet (7)
24 Insurance policy payment (7)
25 Political group (5)

DOWN

1 Muffle, suppress (6)
2 Insects told to 'fly away home' (9)
3 Person now living and working abroad (5)
4 Cigarette flickings (3)
5 Chinwagged (7)
6 Printing fluid (3)
7 Nakedness (6)
11 Red cosmetic powder (5)
13 Meet face to face (9)
15 Surname of singer Gwen (7)
16 Circus tent (3,3)
17 Nourishing and filling (meal) (6)
20 Tear into shreds (3,2)
22 Animal very like a human (3)
23 Traffic snarl-up (3)

ACROSS

1 Use up (7)
5 Scented flower with thorns (4)
10 Female chicken (3)
11 Spread over a wide area (9)
12 Unfit, bungling (5)
13 Warm up again (6)
15 Take on (staff) (6)
17 First name of Swedish TV personality Ms Jonsson (6)
18 Mischa ___, star of The OC (6)
20 Mean, unkind (5)
23 High-ranking police officer (9)
24 Bud Abbott and ___ Costello, comedy duo (3)
25 Manufactured (4)
26 Sportsman's leg protector (4,3)

DOWN

2 Small weight (5)
3 Fond of sugary things (5-7)
4 Car engine (5)
6 Japanese art of paper-folding (7)
7 On any occasion (4)
8 Flourished, prospered (7)
9 Over a considerable period of time (2,3,4,3)
14 Ancient Egyptian writing material (7)
16 Complimented (7)
19 V-shaped nick (5)
21 Spicy tomato sauce or dip (5)
22 Brother of ex-Oasis guitarist Noel Gallagher (4)

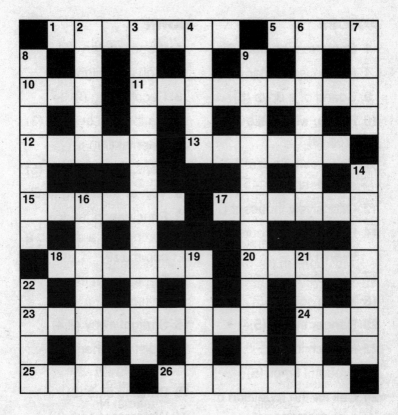

ACROSS

1 Bring from abroad (6)
4 Mark over a letter (6)
9 Sound of a dove (3)
10 People who settle an area (9)
11 Person who poses for an artist (5)
12 Offensively indecent (7)
14 Progress in a course of study (11)
17 Occasional aches (7)
18 Young soldier (5)
20 Danger signal (5,4)
22 Male child (3)
23 Dreadful smell (6)
24 Call for the repetition of a performance (6)

DOWN

1 Wages, salary (6)
2 High and mighty (5)
3 Recollecting (9)
5 Tin for food or drink (3)
6 Oriental (7)
7 Sense in the mouth (5)
8 Vein or artery, eg (5,6)
13 Punctuation mark comprising a dot and a comma (9)
15 General weather pattern (7)
16 Straight away (2,4)
17 Moisture when weeping (5)
19 Dancing club (5)
21 Waterproof coat (3)

THE Sun

ACROSS

7 Traditional writing implement (8,3)

8 Means of acknowledging a superior officer (6)

9 Stroll in the countryside (6)

10 Expressions of approval (8)

11 Costly (4)

12 ___ Fisher, Aussie actress (4)

14 Confirmed, verified (4,4)

17 Bony cavity in the hip area (6)

19 Lower ground between hills (6)

20 Small room equipped for cooking (11)

DOWN

1 Illicit romance (6)

2 Residential areas on the outskirts of towns (8)

3 *Sesame* ___, kids' TV programme (6)

4 Fruits such as limes and oranges (6)

5 Junk emails (4)

6 East ___, Norfolk's region (6)

11 Unfrequented and bleak (8)

13 Underhand, cunning (6)

14 ___ Barton, actress in *St Trinian's* and *The OC* (6)

15 Leaping off a swimming pool board (6)

16 Keanu ___, US actor (6)

18 Participate in an election (4)

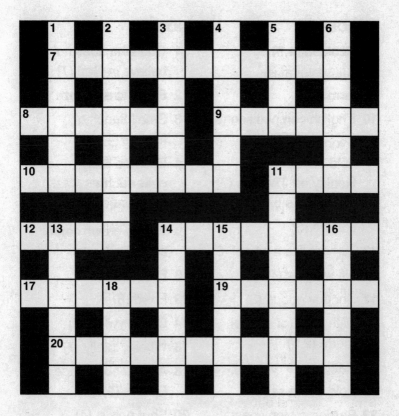

23 (Letters, etc) page ...
Victoria (3,4) ...

20 (Jack-in-...) (7)
21 Airy-fairy dancer (7)

ACROSS

7 Scolded (4,3)

9 American cattle farm (5)

10 English composition (5)

11 Event such as that held annually at Henley-on-Thames (7)

12 Sauce used in oriental cuisine (3)

13 Turning like a wheel (8)

16 Lift weights (4,4)

17 Shoddy goods (3)

19 With bath (of a hotel room) (2,5)

21 Hangman's rope (5)

22 Bold, fearless (5)

23 Barrier to stop coastal flooding (3,4)

DOWN

1 One who does not believe in God (7)

2 Reply to a sneeze (5,3)

3 Small bunch of flowers (4)

4 Become more cheerful (8)

5 Single element (4)

6 Widely grown cereal crop (5)

8 First of all (3,8)

13 Fixed (8)

14 Countrywide (8)

15 Wholly, totally (7)

18 Annual horse race at Epsom (5)

20 Shut noisily (4)

21 At no great distance (4)

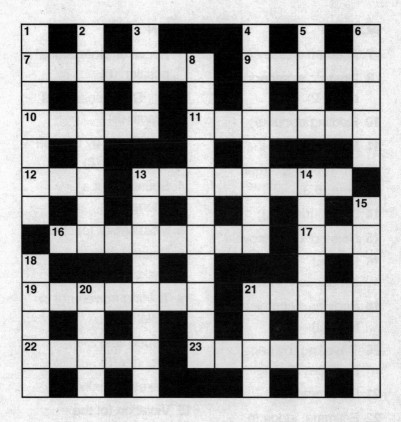

ACROSS

7 Academic essay (6)

8 Lipstick, eyeshadow etc (4-2)

10 Fiddling about (9)

11 Mafia boss (3)

12 Move over a larger area (6,3)

14 Chum, friend (3)

15 Noise of disapproval (3)

16 Prevent congestion (4,5)

18 Body part containing a lobe (3)

20 Travelling (by car, perhaps) (2,3,4)

21 Quite cold (6)

22 Estimate, judge to be (6)

DOWN

1 Social or professional position (6)

2 ___ DiCaprio, star of *Titanic* (8)

3 Line made by the sea on a shore (8)

4 Sounded (of a phone) (4)

5 Most senior teacher (4)

6 Related to the backbone (6)

9 Twirling movement in ballet (9)

13 Issued with a voucher (8)

14 Bakes partially (3-5)

15 Violation (of the peace) (6)

17 Mouse or rat, eg (6)

19 Surprise attack (4)

20 Night birds (4)

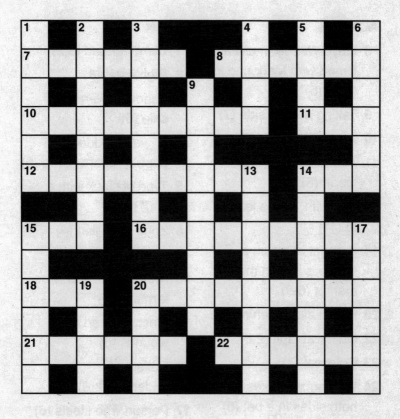

ACROSS

8 Lloyd Webber musical filmed with Madonna in 1996 (5)

9 Taking neither side (7)

10 Australian bush (7)

11 Australian tree-climbing 'bear' (5)

12 ___ with, writes letters to (11)

14 Amount at which a house is put on the market (6,5)

20 Pulled along behind (5)

22 Guilty, at fault (2,5)

23 Colossal (7)

24 With equal stakes on both sides in a bet (5)

DOWN

1 Climb aboard (3,2)

2 Righteous (8)

3 School fund-raising sale (6)

4 ___ and ladders, popular board-game (6)

5 Type of clock with a bird! (6)

6 Zone or region (4)

7 Desolate (5)

13 Announces openly or formally (8)

15 Tincture used on wounds (6)

16 Collect or understand (6)

17 Person who steals (6)

18 Prim and proper (5)

19 Break off, stop (5)

21 Feeble person (4)

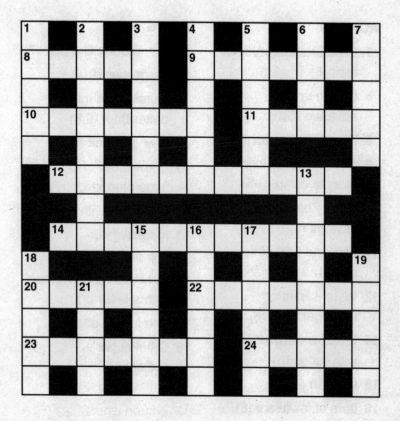

ACROSS

1 Creature preserved in rock (6)

5 Cough up in advance (6)

8 Block of concrete (4)

9 Of a party, lasting from dusk to dawn (3-5)

10 Money earned on savings (8)

11 Ebb and flow of the sea (4)

12 Waist-slimming undergarment (6)

14 Window cleaner's item with rungs (6)

16 Minicab (4)

18 Item of jewellery (8)

20 Answer to a problem (8)

21 Entrance to a room (4)

22 Growing old (6)

23 Number of players in a hockey team (6)

DOWN

2 ___ Bloom, film star (7)

3 Large sword (5)

4 Outstrip, be much better than (5,8)

5 Flying permit (6,7)

6 Thrown out of accommodation (7)

7 Throbbed with pain (5)

13 Incentives or impulses (7)

15 Put inside an envelope with a letter (7)

17 The length of (5)

19 Gatekeeper's cottage (5)

ACROSS

1 Hollywood award (5)

4 Details of where someone lives (7)

9 Puts on the market again (8)

10 Wild hog (4)

11 Fit in a particular environment (6)

12 Remarked, observed (5)

13 Pointer on a clock (4)

15 Grain used for American whiskey (3)

16 Karate blow (4)

17 Bake (meat) in the oven (5)

19 One who skips school (6)

21 Sudden jerk (4)

22 Very quickly (2,2,4)

23 Astounded (7)

24 Unrefined (oil) (5)

DOWN

2 Straining vessel (5)

3 Do a bunk (7)

5 Cleansing to remove germs (12)

6 Mechanical person (5)

7 Unnamed person (2-3-2)

8 Food refusal as a protest (6,6)

14 Place to catch a plane (7)

16 Shop's serving table (7)

18 ___ Towers, Staffordshire theme park (5)

20 Called, christened (5)

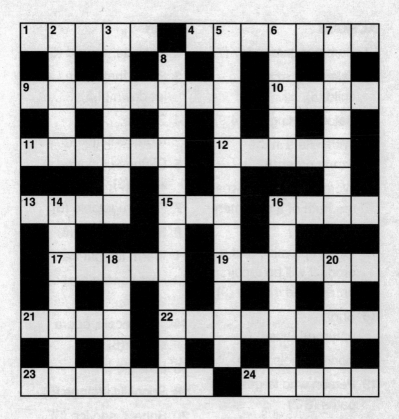

ACROSS

1 Summer garden toy (7)
5 Take as your own child (5)
9 Baton-twirling girl (4,9)
10 With letters in the wrong order (8)
11 Words spoken to swear the truth of a statement in court (4)
12 Written promise that a product will be repaired or replaced if faulty (9)
16 Short upturned (nose) (4)
17 Boring a hole in (8)
19 Person who forges new paths (6-7)
21 Outmoded (5)
22 Making fun of (7)

DOWN

2 Anxious, scared (6)
3 Event that proves a let-down (4,5)
4 Picture, representation (5)
6 Clothes-colouring liquid (3)
7 Root vegetable (6)
8 Sewing thread (6)
11 Warm top garments (9)
13 Fast-flowing part of a river (6)
14 ___ Bocelli, opera singer (6)
15 Invisible (6)
18 Spookily strange (5)
20 Benefit, service (3)

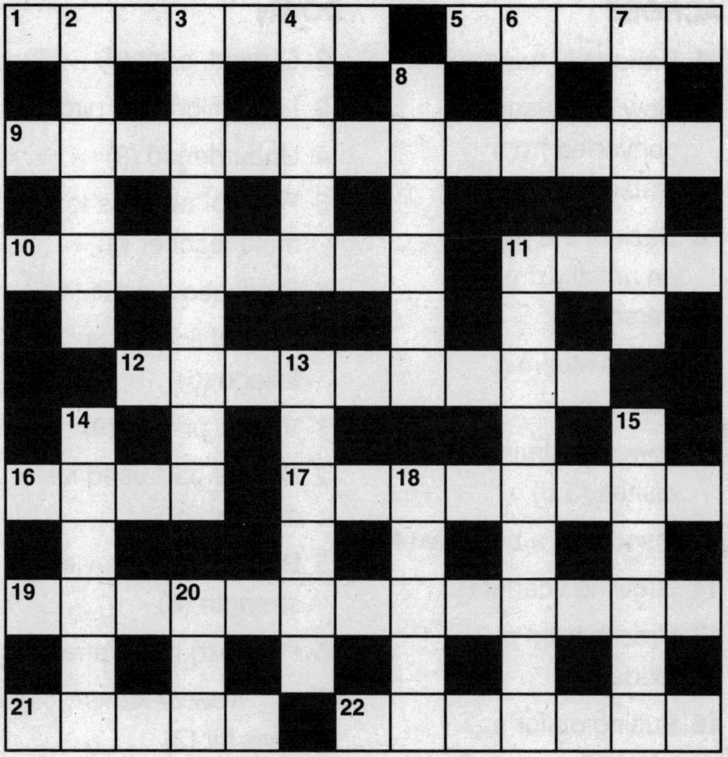

ACROSS

1 Extremely hungry (8)

6 Row of houses converted from stables (4)

8 Back of the neck or an untidily dressed person (6)

9 Boat's steering blade (6)

10 Towel for drying dishes (3,5)

13 Insect like a butterfly (4)

14 Growing scarlet (9)

17 Crossbar on a ladder (4)

18 Putting off for a while (8)

19 Popular variety of seafood (6)

21 Food eaten by pandas (6)

23 Body's blood carrier (4)

24 Hard up (for cash) (8)

DOWN

2 Curved, bent (6)

3 Large flightless bird (3)

4 Unburdened (9)

5 Form of address to a male teacher (3)

6 Produced a profit (4,5)

7 Ring of flowers or foliage (6)

11 Vicars, priests (9)

12 Bicycle part used for steering (9)

15 Bodily tissue providing strength (6)

16 Put (text) into cipher (6)

20 ___ *Now or Never*, Elvis hit (3)

22 Floor-swabbing implement (3)

ACROSS

1 Exclude, leave out (4)
4 Having too little to eat (8)
8 ___ and save, economise (6)
9 Put the ball into play at tennis (6)
10 Building and land producing food (4)
11 Aristocracy (8)
13 Stubbornness (3-10)
16 Puts at risk (8)
19 Plan or scheme formed in the mind (4)
20 Timber fungus (3,3)
22 First name shared by actresses Jensen and Tisdale (6)
23 Overdrawn at a bank (2,3,3)
24 Go upwards (4)

DOWN

2 System of parts working together (9)
3 Complete victory or success (7)
4 Loosen (a brooch) (5)
5 Put out of action (7)
6 Of the countryside (5)
7 Bible's first woman (3)
12 Bland, without flavour (9)
14 One who flies planes (7)
15 Word often accompanied by 'nor' (7)
17 This planet (5)
18 Burn with hot water (5)
21 Sprinted (3)

ACROSS

1 Part of a foot or shoe (4)
4 Painted cloth at the rear of a stage (8)
8 Break out of jail (6)
9 Be sorry about (6)
10 White and yellow food items (4)
11 Hitting (flies) (8)
13 Nocturnal meal (8,5)
16 Christina ___, American singer, songwriter and actress (8)
19 *The ___ Duckling*, fairy tale (4)
20 Begin hostilities (6)
22 Determined, purposeful (6)
23 Rendezvous, get-togethers (8)
24 ___ hour, busy traffic time (4)

DOWN

2 Laid-back (4-5)
3 Connection, collaboration (7)
4 ___ you, words said after a sneeze (5)
5 Small dried grape used when baking (7)
6 Finger or number (5)
7 First number (3)
12 Baby birds (9)
14 Small cucumber used for pickling (7)
15 Line round the world on a map (7)
17 Unfitting (5)
18 Also known as (5)
21 Part of the foot (3)

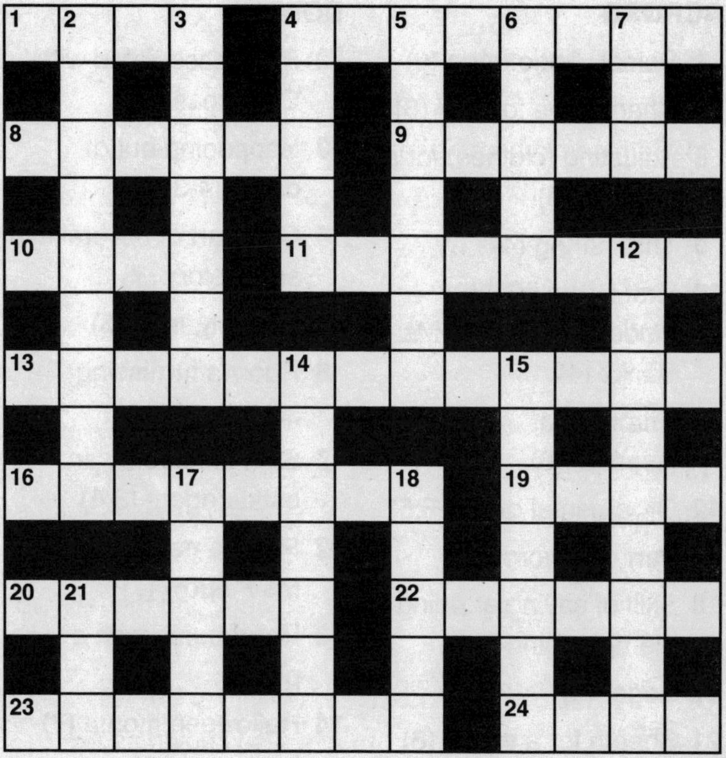

ACROSS

1 Select, settle upon (6)

5 Change the form of (6)

8 Adjusting (clothes) for a better fit (8)

9 Thick string (4)

10 First name of US model and actress Ms Banks (4)

11 Eruption (of disease) (8)

12 Ornamental dwarf (6,5)

15 Part of a word (8)

18 Skill of saying or doing the right thing (4)

20 Eager (4)

21 Sheath for a sword (8)

22 Rude, saucy (6)

23 Insect with pincer-like claws (6)

DOWN

2 Plant associated with Christmas (5)

3 Happening out of doors (4-3)

4 One part of several in a serial story (7)

5 Possibly, may (5)

6 Room's furnishing scheme (5)

7 Sign erected by an estate agent (3,4)

12 First name of actress Ms Paltrow (7)

13 Hand-bomb with a pin (7)

14 Halloween month (7)

16 Move forward aggressively (5)

17 Thick, shaggy (hair) (5)

19 Royal dog (5)

ACROSS

7 Personal cleanliness (7)

9 Chelmsford's county (5)

10 Colour of hearts in a pack of cards (3)

11 In the first place (3,1,5)

12 Friend (5)

14 Portion of food at a meal (7)

16 Made from pottery (7)

18 Roll of tobacco leaves for smoking (5)

19 Small pruning-shears (9)

20 Costa ___ Sol, Spanish holiday region (3)

21 Soft leather with a rough surface (5)

22 Betrayal of one's country (7)

DOWN

1 Angel-like (8)

2 Grew old (4)

3 Church tower (6)

4 Ferret-like animal (6)

5 Breaking out of jail (8)

6 Motorway leaving point (4)

8 World's surface (6,5)

13 Indicated the route to (8)

15 Making a bubbling sound (8)

17 Complain under the breath (6)

18 Small jewellery case (6)

19 Neither great nor that bad (2-2)

20 Slang for 'money' (4)

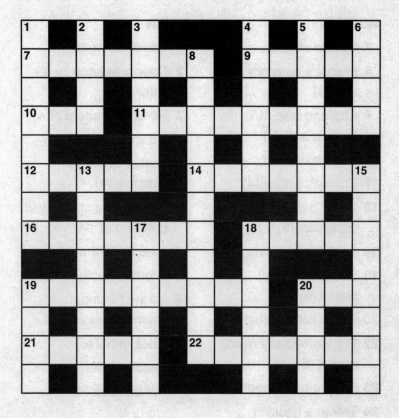

ACROSS

7 Get rid of (5,3)

8 France's currency unit (4)

9 City and lake of Switzerland (6)

10 Compass point (5)

11 Bookie's prices (4)

12 Letter panel on a computer (8)

14 Loch Ness' country (8)

18 Small piece in chess (4)

20 Clean with a brush (5)

22 Put (someone's mind) at rest (6)

23 Soothing ointment (4)

24 Talk in a choking manner (8)

DOWN

1 Cotton string (6)

2 County famous for its cider (8)

3 Return or retreat (2,4)

4 Mean, miserly (6)

5 Yogi or Pooh, for example (4)

6 Person who shoots with bow and arrows (6)

13 Directly contrary (8)

15 Informal (clothes) (6)

16 Taking the most optimistic view (2,4)

17 Fatal, lethal (6)

19 Distorted (6)

21 Cut of steak (4)

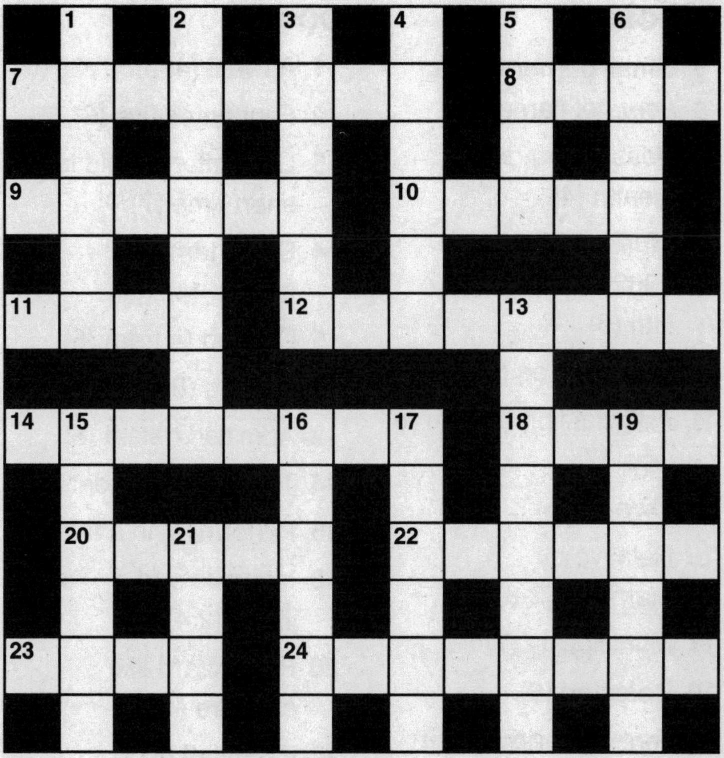

ACROSS

7 Small burner with a very hot flame (8)

8 Possessing great wealth (4)

9 *Mutiny on the* ___, 1962 Marlon Brando film (6)

10 Ballerina, eg (6)

11 Artificial fibre similar to wool (7)

13 Own up (5)

15 Relative by marriage (2-3)

17 Municipality (7)

19 Defeated (6)

21 Tree-lined drive or road (6)

23 Runner ___, vegetable (4)

24 Moves like a worm (8)

DOWN

1 As well (4)

2 Four times five (6)

3 Look after a child for a short time (7)

4 Slang term for 'potato' (4)

5 Clipped (a tree) (6)

6 Plotting (8)

12 Admitted defeat (8)

14 Tending to wander (7)

16 Performing in a film (6)

18 Nervous and jittery (2,4)

20 Pond lizard-like creature (4)

22 Exploited (4)

ACROSS

6 Small passenger vehicle (7)

7 Instrument with black and white keys (5)

9 Melodious bird (4)

10 Got in a flap (8)

11 Be quietly furious (6)

13 Chilly (4)

15 Items for hanging up washing (4)

16 Impolitely enquiring into someone's private life (6)

18 Drop missiles from a plummeting aircraft (4-4)

21 Street (4)

22 Burp (5)

23 Angry and deliberately unfriendly (7)

DOWN

1 Ultimate, last (5)

2 Ill health (8)

3 Tyre inflating device (4)

4 Flat circular object (4)

5 Cover by wrapping (7)

8 One of the Seven Dwarfs (6)

12 Boss, familiarly (3,3)

13 Builder's hard-setting floor substance (8)

14 Made healthy and strong again (7)

17 Series of tennis strokes (5)

19 Every one (4)

20 Hardback or paperback (4)

ACROSS

1 Eligible for being paid back (10)
8 One of the five Great Lakes (5)
9 Cocker or springer, for example (7)
10 Be subjected to, suffer (7)
11 Backbone (5)
12 Learner, rookie (9)
15 Name of seven Stuart kings of Scotland (5)
17 Start a voyage (3,4)
19 Neither here nor there (2,5)
20 Prize for merit (5)
21 School's midday break (10)

DOWN

2 Sinned (5)
3 Fluster, rattle (7)
4 Cut-price shop (8,5)
5 Gold-coloured metal alloy (5)
6 Version of a book (7)
7 Colour associated with sadness (4)
8 Drag along (4)
12 Placed bets (7)
13 Person rejected by society (7)
14 Glided along (4)
15 Link up (4)
16 Simple character from a nursery rhyme (5)
18 Awakening clock (5)

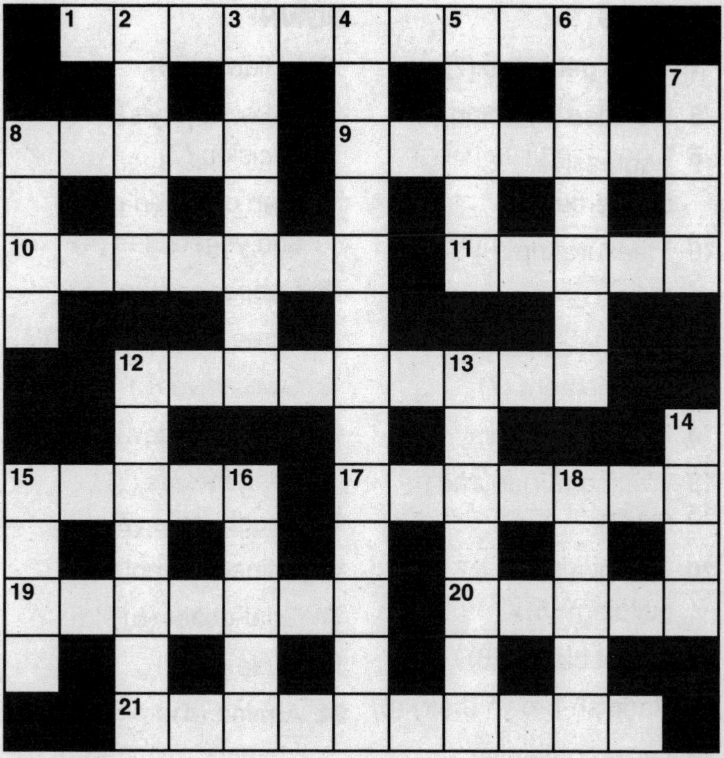
1
2
3
4
5
6
7
8
9
10
11
12
13
14
15
16
17
18
19
20
21

ACROSS

1 Try to get votes (7)
5 Included in, within (5)
9 Aggressive, dangerous (6)
10 Pleasure trip (6)
11 Group of singers (5)
12 Keep in solitary confinement (7)
14 In an elegant way (9)
18 Wafting (air) to and fro (7)
20 Remove (from a building) (5)
22 Sweet biscuit (6)
23 Reddish-brown (hair) (6)
24 Items containing greetings (5)
25 Thin sheets of fine wood used for decorating furniture (7)

DOWN

2 In flames (6)
3 In law, a jury's decision (7)
4 Dish of boiled meat and vegetables (4)
6 Copper or steel (5)
7 Three times thirty (6)
8 Own, have (7)
13 Very small towel for washing (7)
15 Cuddly, cute (7)
16 Chinese temple (6)
17 Goal-getter (6)
19 Nude (5)
21 Arrived (4)

ACROSS

1 Ending in death (5)
4 Opposite of 'big' (5)
9 Change for the better (6)
10 Show, uncover (6)
12 Happy state (13)
13 Submissive person who gets trampled on (7)
18 Outwit easily (3,5,5)
19 Delay, postpone (3,3)
20 Food cupboard (6)
21 Machine's humming sound (5)
22 Irish county whose main town is Tralee (5)

DOWN

2 Be present at (6)
3 Fall out in a friendly way (5,2,6)
5 Union between people of different religions or race (5,8)
6 Make slack (6)
7 Popular large house plant (5)
8 Honking farmyard birds (5)
11 Space for keeping spare things (7)
14 Violently explode (volcano) (5)
15 Telltale (6)
16 Kill, slaughter (6)
17 Love intensely (5)

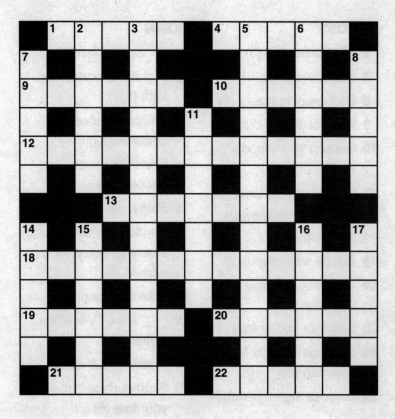

ACROSS

3 Worthless dog (3)

7 Beat out (corn) (6)

8 Ran away to marry (6)

9 Front claw of a crab (6)

10 Supplying weapons to (6)

11 Blood-curdling (5-8)

13 (Said) with humorous intention (6-2-5)

18 Gentle walk (6)

19 Sherlock ___, fictional detective (6)

20 Sport for two or four (6)

21 Package brought by the postman (6)

22 Distress signal (inits)(3)

DOWN

1 Small shellfish (6)

2 Signalling or warning light (6)

3 Without interesting features (13)

4 Bonds between people (13)

5 Stuffy, official (6)

6 Beatle after whom Liverpool's airport is named (6)

11 Take (an exam) (3)

12 ___ Wan, TV fashion stylist (3)

14 Retail ___, shop (6)

15 Solid surface beneath your feet (6)

16 First name shared by actresses Ms Duff and Ms Swank (6)

17 Small round opening in a sail or shoe for rope or a lace to go through (6)

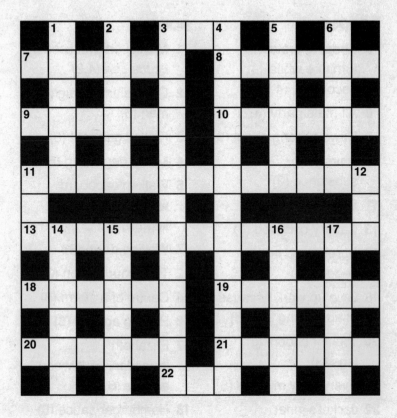

ACROSS

5 Sheet to protect furniture while decorating (4,5)

8 All-male party (4,2)

9 Dawdle, hang about (6)

10 Hairstyling substance (3)

11 Stir up, provoke (6)

13 Canary-coloured (6)

15 Shrub used in hedges (6)

18 Give up work because of advancing age (6)

20 Tool for chopping logs (3)

21 Every sixty minutes (6)

22 Jacket's inner material (6)

23 Marching to a different beat (3,2,4)

DOWN

1 Martial art practised by Bruce Lee (4,2)

2 Comedian's straight man (6)

3 Knitted garment (6)

4 Lowly, degrading (6)

6 Walk-in cupboard where goods are kept (9)

7 Wolfing down (9)

12 Take court action (3)

14 Centre of a storm (3)

16 Playing against (6)

17 Elizabeth ___, legendary Hollywood actress (6)

18 Hamburger sauce (6)

19 Fuel-carrying lorry or ship (6)

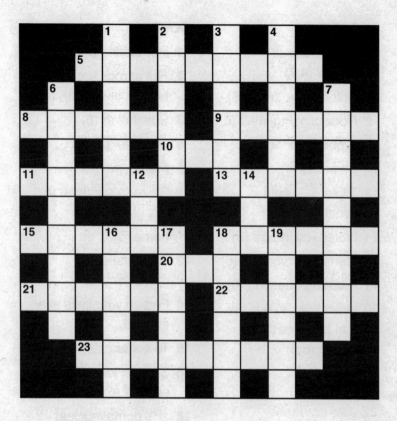

ACROSS

7 Top person at school (4,7)

8 Soft mud or snow (6)

9 Rock-clinging shell (6)

10 Ambassador (8)

11 Statistics (4)

12 Triple ___, field event (4)

14 Increased in size (8)

17 Mention, comment (6)

19 Puzzling question (6)

20 Indications in the sky that bad weather is ahead (5,6)

DOWN

1 Hot-tasting pod (6)

2 Fall of rock from a hillside or cliff (8)

3 Small river (6)

4 Capsule, pill (6)

5 Friend, pal (4)

6 Seize (a criminal) (6)

11 Ate away from home (5,3)

13 Nervousness, discontent (6)

14 Person who lives in an igloo (6)

15 To some extent (6)

16 Sign on for military service (6)

18 ___ bomb, nuclear weapon (4)

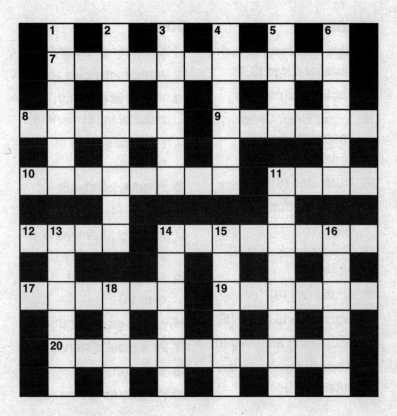

ACROSS

7 Sign indicating a truck's unusual cargo (8,4)

8 Austria's capital (6)

9 ___ of Dock Green, 1950s/60s police series (5)

10 Track laps (8)

13 Noise of shutting a door hard (4)

15 Sheepshank or reef, eg (4)

16 Aimed (at) (8)

17 Warmed and dried (5)

19 Happening annually (6)

21 Good behaviour when eating (5,7)

DOWN

1 Conjurer or wizard (8)

2 Author unknown (4)

3 Player of a church musical instrument (8)

4 Hospital's room of beds (4)

5 Pliable, bendy (8)

6 Agony (4)

11 Kim ___, Samantha in *Sex and the City* (8)

12 Scattering liquid over (8)

14 ___ to say, of course (8)

17 At a great distance (4)

18 Moist (4)

20 A really long time (4)

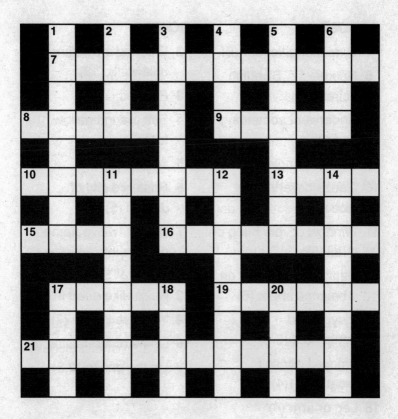

ACROSS

1 Unreasonable fear (6)

5 Noomi ___, Swedish actress (6)

8 Underwent something bad (8)

9 Be at an angle (4)

10 Gauze covering the face (4)

11 Window covers hung on a rail (8)

12 Debit's counterpart on a balance sheet (6)

13 Playground equipment (3-3)

15 Enjoyed oneself greatly (3,1,4)

18 Leg or arm (4)

19 Archaeological sites (4)

20 Marking (the skin) permanently (8)

21 Meeting's list of topics (6)

22 ___ Franklin, singer known as the 'Queen of Soul' (6)

DOWN

2 Entering a dwelling unlawfully (13)

3 Puzzled (7)

4 Soft orange-yellow fruit (7)

5 Jockey (5)

6 Rose-red city of Jordan (5)

7 One of twelve named periods into which a year is divided (8,5)

13 Raisin-like dried fruit (7)

14 Increase in size (7)

16 Crime of fire-raising (5)

17 On the ocean (2,3)

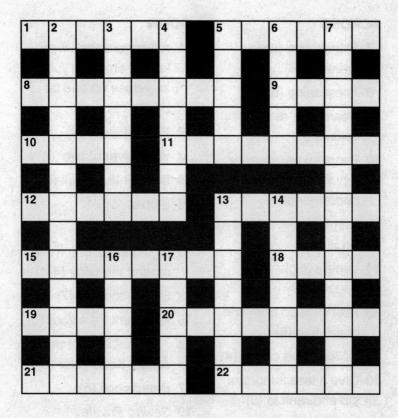

ACROSS

7 Skimpy two-piece swimsuit (6)

8 Possessing (6)

9 Deafening, at a high volume (4)

10 People who interrupt a public speech or performance (8)

11 Come closer, form a circle (6,5)

14 Variety of pie dough (5,6)

18 Fabric made from fine goats' hair (8)

19 Collect (ripe crops) (4)

20 Give a less important job and rank to (6)

21 Rocking crib (6)

DOWN

1 (Of spectacles), with lenses enabling you to see close up and far off (7)

2 Passed away (4)

3 Whichever of two (6)

4 Blanket-like cloak (6)

5 Slopes (8)

6 Furious (5)

12 Light plastic ring twirled around the body (4-4)

13 Syrupy topping (7)

15 Attendant (at a zoo) (6)

16 ___ Brosnan, former James Bond actor (6)

17 Bread cook (5)

19 *Saving Private* ___, Tom Hanks film (4)

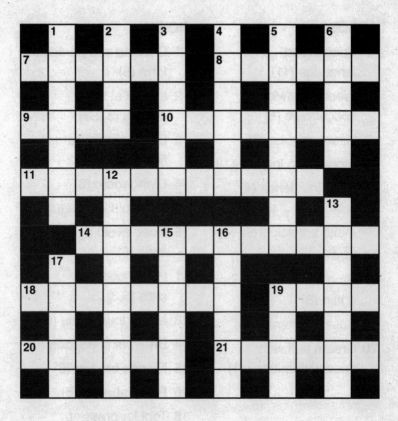

ACROSS

7 Specialised language (11)

8 West Bromwich ___, soccer club (6)

9 Usual, regular (6)

10 Increase in intensity (8)

11 Pillar in a fence (4)

12 Dishonest scheme to make a quick profit (4)

14 Makes by mixing (8)

17 Ring the same number again (6)

19 Solemn promise (6)

20 Cream puff with chocolate sauce (11)

DOWN

1 Designs in a particular form (6)

2 Linked at the elbows (3,2,3)

3 Bright showy garden flower (6)

4 Living room (6)

5 Tip liquid from a jug (4)

6 Road avoiding a town (6)

11 Public booth for calls (5,3)

13 Mysterious, eerie (6)

14 Breed of sheepdog (6)

15 Niece's brother (6)

16 Put a label on (6)

18 Tool for pressing clothes (4)

ACROSS

1 Step-sibling (4-7)
9 Sound that has been copied (4,9)
10 Mutinied (8)
12 Fruit skin (4)
14 Steam bath (5)
15 Smelling mouldy (5)
19 List of duties (4)
20 Smooth greasy healing preparation for the skin (8)
22 Place where valuables may be securely stored (6,7)
24 Rude, impolite (3-8)

DOWN

2 Electrical unit (3)
3 Fields used for growing crops or raising livestock (8)
4 Wealthier (6)
5 House in Gone with the Wind (4)
6 Point of origin of an earthquake (9)
7 Fable or fairy tale (5)
8 Quick on your feet (5)
11 Pretty, lovely (9)
13 Numerous, of many parts (8)
16 Top of a wave (5)
17 Concealed, obscured (6)
18 Nation, country (5)
21 Part of a plant (4)
23 Container for return postage (inits)(3)

S*un*

ACROSS

1 Unusual objects or facts (11)

9 Tiny child (3)

10 Best Supporting Actor Oscar winner in *Dallas Buyers Club* (5,4)

11 Easy-going (8)

12 Heroine of *Doctor Zhivago* (4)

14 Starting point (6)

16 Extremely busy (6)

18 Mimic, imitate (4)

19 From the US (8)

22 Take legal action against (9)

23 Sick (3)

24 Investigation of plants and animals at school (6,5)

DOWN

2 To the time when (5)

3 Wounds (8)

4 Length of twine (6)

5 Arrange neatly (4)

6 Refined, graceful (7)

7 Instrument used to listen to the heart or lungs (11)

8 Cylindrical firework (5,6)

13 Marquee where ale can be bought (4,4)

15 Starchy milk pudding (7)

17 Having natural protection from a disease (6)

20 Sobbed (5)

21 Restaurant list (4)

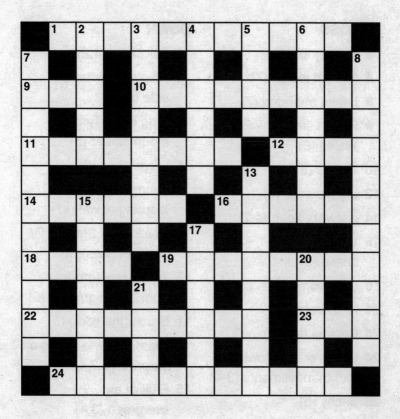

ACROSS

1 Easy (job) (5)
4 Not yet tested (7)
8 Leave stranded (7)
9 Patron saint of Wales (5)
10 Opens (a door) (7)
12 Light purple (5)
14 Not very keen (4-7)
18 Venomous UK snake (5)
19 Carnivorous fish (7)
21 Hi there! (5)
23 Canvas bag (7)
24 Interpret by following mouth movements (3-4)
25 Bitchy (5)

DOWN

1 Fall silent (4,2)
2 Ship's right-hand side (9)
3 Sing like a Tyrolean mountaineer (5)
4 Large vase (3)
5 Young child just learning to walk (7)
6 *Coronation Street*'s TV channel (inits)(3)
7 Take away (money) from a total amount (6)
11 Brush (the floor) (5)
13 Hide, ready to cause a surprise (3,2,4)
15 Fruit of an evergreen (3,4)
16 Jennifer Aniston's character in *Friends* (6)
17 ___ sugar, amber-coloured sweet (6)
20 Item from the past (5)
22 Drink like a dog (3)
23 Owned (3)

ACROSS

1 Ambassador's residence (7)
5 Measurement of land area (4)
10 Also, as well (3)
11 Airport passenger buildings (9)
12 Possibly, perhaps (5)
13 Place where lashes grow (6)
15 Group of sports teams who play each other (6)
17 ___ Bonham Carter, actress (6)
18 Official count of the population (6)
20 ___ Jessica Parker, actress (5)
23 Job undertaken by a nanny (9)
24 Fitting, suitable (3)
25 24-hour periods (4)
26 Suppose (7)

DOWN

2 Sullen, grumpy (5)
3 As an upper limit (2,3,7)
4 Uncontrolled rush (5)
6 Deadly poison (7)
7 Make less difficult (4)
8 Lose your footing (7)
9 Quality of being never-ending (12)
14 Jungle knife (7)
16 Town facility (7)
19 One of a flight of treads (5)
21 Domain, kingdom (5)
22 Citric or sulphuric, for example (4)

ACROSS

1 Expression of approval or agreement (6)

4 Air journey (6)

9 Half of four (3)

10 Ignoring (a temptation) (9)

11 In that place (5)

12 Device for connecting non-matching plugs and sockets (7)

14 From direct personal experience (2,5,4)

17 Cowboy hat (7)

18 Upright and rigid (5)

20 Container for writing fluid (3,6)

22 Black road-surfacing material (3)

23 Steak and ___ pie, common dish (6)

24 (Lead) into sin (6)

DOWN

1 Wily, shrewd (6)

2 Light cake made with sultanas or cheese and served buttered (5)

3 Day-care centres for young children (9)

5 ___ Angeles, Californian city (3)

6 Sparkle like a polished surface (7)

7 Striped big cat (5)

8 Kill (an important person) for political reasons (11)

13 Successful people (9)

15 Nipped, pinched (7)

16 Robust, firmly built (6)

17 Fix with adhesive (5)

19 Come in (5)

21 UK honour or award (inits)(3)

ACROSS

8 Monkey or ape, for example (7)

9 Blemish, defect (5)

10 Melted ice (5)

11 Lowest rank of soldier (7)

12 Costing too much in money or other resources (12)

16 Cloth for wiping your nose (12)

20 Part of a scrum in rugby (4,3)

23 High-pitched cry of a horse (5)

24 *Cracklin'* ___, Neil Diamond hit (5)

25 Stop from happening (7)

DOWN

1 Frogs' eggs (5)

2 Eavesdrop (6,2)

3 Material, cloth (6)

4 Non-permanent member of staff (4)

5 Assert positively (6)

6 Canned fish (4)

7 Pointed tower on a church (7)

13 Word paired with 'neither' (3)

14 Added money to (an account) (8)

15 Fruit grown in sticks (7)

17 Seed within a hard shell (6)

18 Delay, obstruct (6)

19 Colour of snowdrops (5)

21 Teapot insulator (4)

22 Sobbed, cried (4)

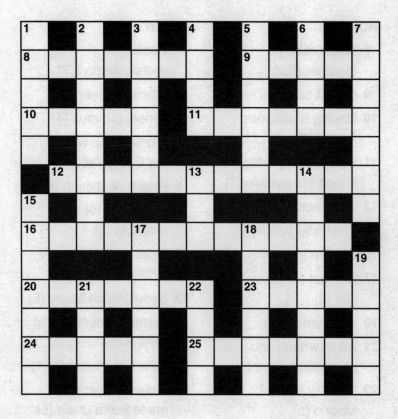

ACROSS

7 Herd (cattle) together (5,2)

9 Crowd-scene actor (5)

10 Having a delicious flavour (5)

11 Range within which things are audible (7)

12 Glide across snow (3)

13 Work-shy people (8)

16 Loosen (a garment) (8)

17 Married woman's title (3)

19 Sweetheart (7)

21 Art of writing and presenting plays (5)

22 Country, capital Madrid (5)

23 Solidify, thicken (7)

DOWN

1 Public demonstration (7)

2 Interrogate (8)

3 Tense, nervous (4)

4 High fur cap worn by the Guards (8)

5 Prickly sensation (4)

6 Spaghetti, for example (5)

8 From a period before written records (11)

13 Speaking unclearly (8)

14 Rushes around out of control (8)

15 As a rule, normally (7)

18 Flower sometimes made into a chain (5)

20 Water around a castle (4)

21 Eat grandly (4)

ACROSS

7 At some future point in time (3,3)

8 Cement, sand and water (6)

10 Law-breaker (9)

11 Young male person (3)

12 Amount gained, after tax (3,6)

14 Because, since (3)

15 Rotter, bounder (3)

16 Attraction such as Disneyland (5,4)

18 Milk treatment process (inits)(3)

20 Remained in the same place (6,3)

21 Murmur of a brook (6)

22 Vehicle fuel (6)

DOWN

1 TV style guru (3,3)

2 Placed (a plant) in another container (8)

3 ___ Thatcher, 1980s PM (8)

4 On ___ marks, pre-race instruction (4)

5 Cigarette butt (4)

6 Plea to God (6)

9 Place for a cappuccino or latte (6,3)

13 Wobbled (8)

14 Trendy 1920s girls (8)

15 Stout, plump (6)

17 Kitchen water boiler (6)

19 Hollow cylinder (4)

20 Common name for sodium chloride (4)

ACROSS

8 Country whose capital is Rome (5)

9 Liquid for hair washing (7)

10 Frightening tidal wave (7)

11 Consent to do something (5)

12 War arena (11)

14 Nausea on board a ship (11)

20 Arrange, make tidy (5)

22 San Francisco's country (7)

23 Portrait, representation (7)

24 Sharp-eyed bird of prey (5)

DOWN

1 Mucky (5)

2 Make very wet (8)

3 Oppressive leader (6)

4 Have high hopes (6)

5 Trip to observe animals in the wild (6)

6 Cowboy's sharp boot extension (4)

7 Sacha Baron ___, creator of Ali G, Borat and Brüno (5)

13 Details of broadcasting, arts and entertainment (8)

15 Burial cloth (6)

16 Hole on the Moon (6)

17 Lacked, wanted (6)

18 Lathery, sudsy (5)

19 (Had) consumed (5)

21 Set of cards (4)

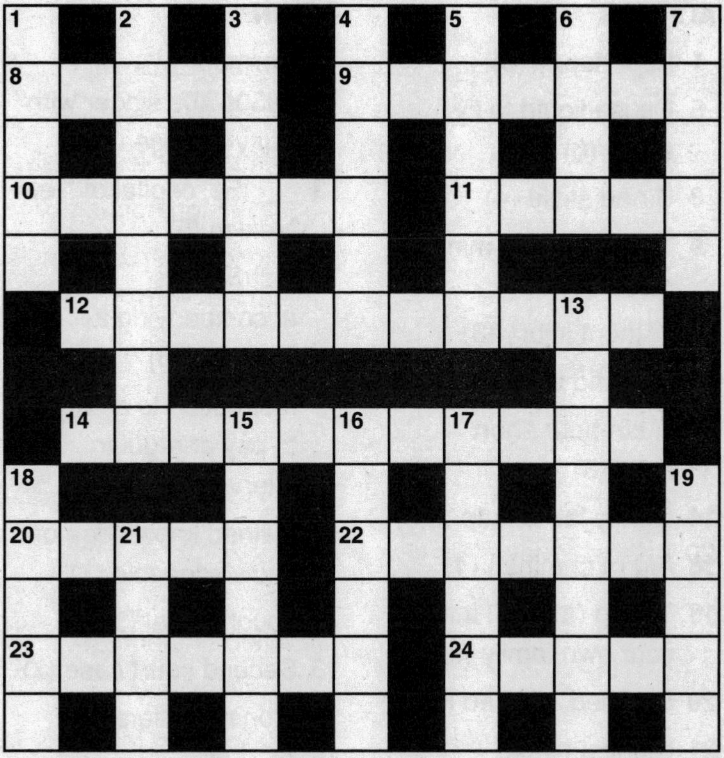
1
2
3
4
5
6
7
8
9
10
11
12
13
14
15
16
17
18
19
20
21
22
23
24

ACROSS

1 Kept happy (6)
5 Cause liquid to fly about (6)
8 Broad smile (4)
9 Title-guessing mime game (8)
10 Without injury (8)
11 ___ and void, invalid (4)
12 Rush-hour short cut (3,3)
14 Gently fall asleep (3,3)
16 Aid (a criminal) (4)
18 Taking (a child) into your own family (8)
20 Soothed, calmed (8)
21 Highest single number (4)
22 Common cause of hay fever (6)
23 Buy back from pawn (6)

DOWN

2 Carmen ___, 1930s/40s singer with fruity headgear (7)
3 ___ Fe, capital of New Mexico (5)
4 Instructions accompanying a product (13)
5 Instruction to a bank to pay at regular intervals (8,5)
6 Gained knowledge or knowledgeable (7)
7 Tough metal (5)
13 Second court case (7)
15 Money matters (7)
17 Shout from an appreciative audience (5)
19 Lean and muscular, but not bulky (5)

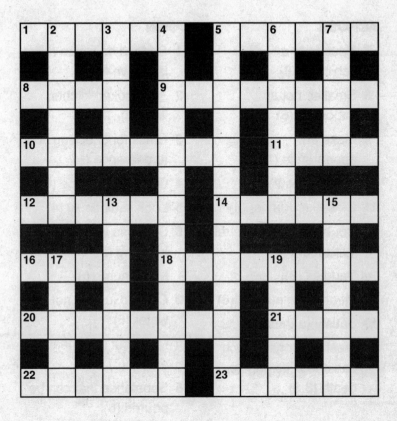

ACROSS

7 Nausea in a vehicle (3-8)

8 Smaller, not as important (6)

9 Make an appearance (4,2)

10 Asked (about) (8)

11 Closed (curtains) (4)

12 Double-reed orchestral instrument (4)

14 Baddies (8)

17 Meal eaten outside (6)

19 Satisfy (a thirst) (6)

20 Freshwater fish which can shock its prey to death (8,3)

DOWN

1 Surface on which a film is shown (6)

2 ___ cooker, kitchen item (8)

3 Glass for checking your appearance (6)

4 Glided across ice (6)

5 Look squintingly (4)

6 Suppose without knowing (6)

11 Made numb (8)

13 Cooked in very hot water (6)

14 Move out from, leave empty (6)

15 Substance that can be poured (6)

16 ___ Kidman, actress (6)

18 Requirement (4)

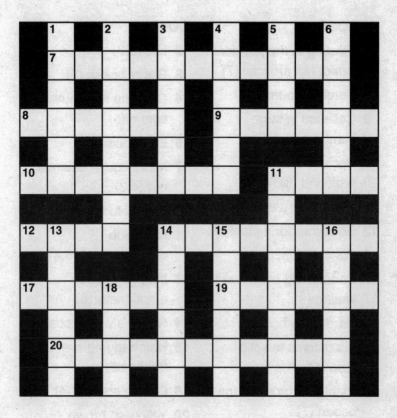

ACROSS

1 Existing in the physical world, not artificial (7)

5 Cardiff's country (5)

9 Collapse in large numbers (4,4,5)

10 Became more profound (8)

11 Number in a quartet (4)

12 Container for a plant (9)

16 Put out of focus (4)

17 Concerning books and writing (8)

19 Hardly any? (4,2,7)

21 Accustoms to solid food (5)

22 Plant that grows in the ocean (7)

DOWN

2 Lilo (3,3)

3 Out of favour (9)

4 Creature from outer space (5)

6 Each one (3)

7 Make equal, balance out (4,2)

8 Painful to touch (6)

11 Nightclub entertainment (5,4)

13 Indulge oneself emotionally (6)

14 Sheep's woolly coat (6)

15 Hair hanging over the forehead (6)

18 Choice steak (1-4)

20 Yellowish-brown colour (3)

ACROSS

1 In all likelihood (8)
6 Detest (4)
8 ___ and Hardy, early film comedians (6)
9 Person who avoids work or other duties (6)
10 Football's opposite of attacker (8)
13 Measure of length (4)
14 Veered from side to side (9)
17 Trip to visit places (4)
18 Relating to home matters (8)
19 Baggage handler (6)
21 Not very wide (6)
23 Colour-stained (4)
24 Ready-to-eat meals (4,4)

DOWN

2 Rose onto the hind legs (6)
3 Metal rod (3)
4 Levelled and cleared (ground) (9)
5 Opposite of 'no' (3)
6 Hirsute quality (9)
7 Deep ditch (6)
11 Went to live abroad (9)
12 Army units (9)
15 Country that is ruled by another country (6)
16 Loose Japanese robe (6)
20 One of the armed services (inits)(3)
22 Umpire in a football match (3)

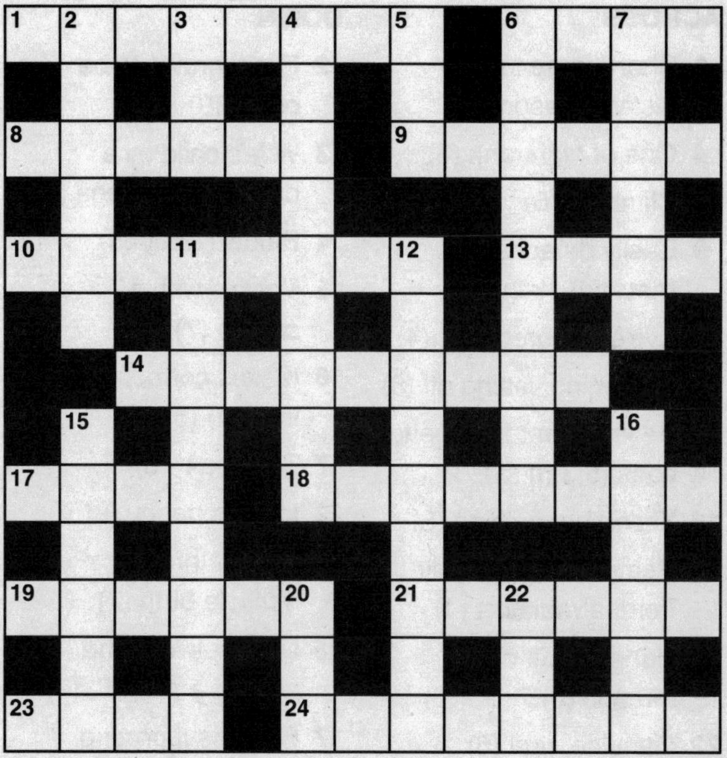

ACROSS

1 Short name for the festive season (4)

4 One of high rank (8)

8 Climb up (6)

9 Easily detachable (necktie) (4-2)

10 Eye's coloured part (4)

11 Pardoning, letting off (8)

13 Be impatient for time to pass (5,3,5)

16 Escorting, guiding (8)

19 Removed trapped air from (a radiator) (4)

20 Hanging tuft of threads (6)

22 Genuine, real (6)

23 Diminished in quantity (8)

24 Outdoor swimming pool (4)

DOWN

2 Fungi grown to be eaten (9)

3 Wife's child by a previous marriage (7)

4 Elbow gently (5)

5 Vehicle with a saddle (7)

6 Makes corrections to (text) (5)

7 Time past (3)

12 Infant's nanny (9)

14 One of three at a multiple birth (7)

15 Descriptive of the path of a satellite (7)

17 Frame supporting a picture during painting (5)

18 ___ Prix, famous motor race (5)

21 Old name for beer (3)

ACROSS

1 Sentimentally cute (4)
4 Brushing (a horse) (8)
8 Settled an argument and became friends (4,2)
9 Most modern and up-to-date (6)
10 Jumping insect (4)
11 Speaking slowly and lazily (8)
13 Being developed or prepared (2,3,8)
16 Puts into quarantine (8)
19 Lead singer of U2 (4)
20 Heat or friendliness (6)
22 Allow (6)
23 Person pretending to be another (8)
24 Toy on a string (2-2)

DOWN

2 Feeble people (9)
3 Hair around the organ of sight (7)
4 Stared open-mouthed (5)
5 Old-fashioned light (3,4)
6 Drivers' stopover (5)
7 UK's medical organisation (inits)(3)
12 Unimportant person (9)
14 Random bullet fired (3,4)
15 Freedom, release from captivity (7)
17 Style of dancing which involves a low bar (5)
18 Really good (5)
21 Provide weapons to (3)

ACROSS

1 Hanging spike formed from freezing dripping water (6)

5 Make a difference to (6)

8 Appropriate, to the point (8)

9 Large brass instrument (4)

10 Turn round fast (4)

11 Boxer's heavy sack for hitting (8)

12 Unlikely to linger in the memory (11)

15 Put things away at the end of the working day (6,2)

18 Requiring little effort (4)

20 Unconscious state (4)

21 Gradually decreased (8)

22 Complaint, or game bird (6)

23 Belgium's continent (6)

DOWN

2 Low-priced (5)

3 Less dirty (7)

4 Typical specimen (7)

5 ___ Villa, Midlands soccer club (5)

6 Go and get (5)

7 Green leafy vegetable (7)

12 Quality or feature of food (7)

13 Lean cut of rump beef (7)

14 Liquidiser (7)

16 ___ Reeves, *Speed* star (5)

17 Avoid, sidestep (5)

19 Ewes and rams (5)

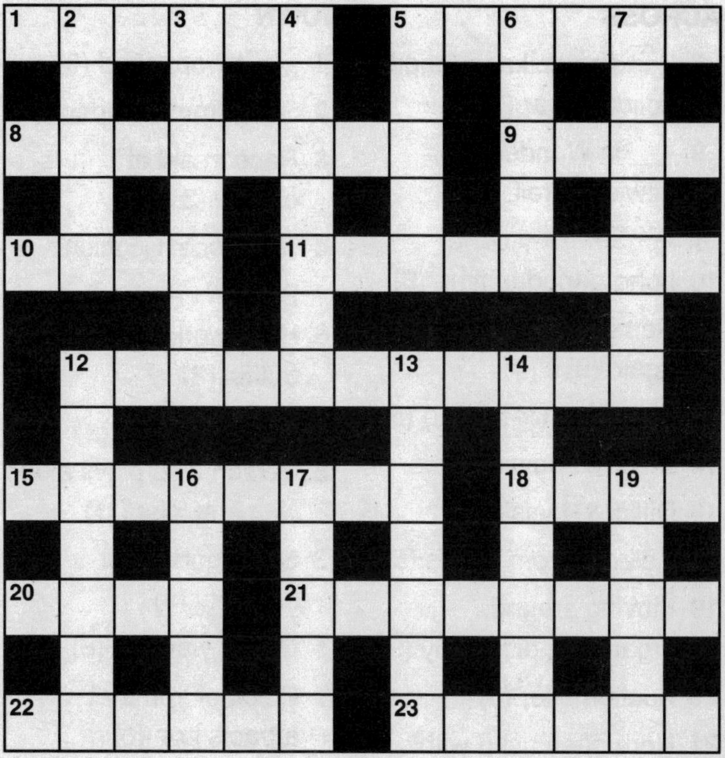

ACROSS

7 ___ shorts, knee-length holiday gear (7)

9 ___ in Wonderland, Lewis Carroll character (5)

10 Long period of time (3)

11 Remember on seeing again (9)

12 Occupied (of a seat) (5)

14 Enigma, puzzle (7)

16 Difficult decision (7)

18 Release from bonds (5)

19 Moving around, organising differently (9)

20 Auction offer (3)

21 Herb often used with parsley in stuffing (5)

22 Nervous strain (7)

DOWN

1 ___ to, opposed (8)

2 Song from an opera (4)

3 Race in aid of charity (3,3)

4 Traditional Scottish dish (6)

5 Hard-working, dutiful (8)

6 This place (4)

8 Person who plays along with a soloist (11)

13 Spoilsports, wet blankets (8)

15 Giving way (to) (8)

17 Piece of iron that attracts iron (6)

18 Requiring immediate action (6)

19 Speed at which something moves or changes (4)

20 Food used to trap animals (4)

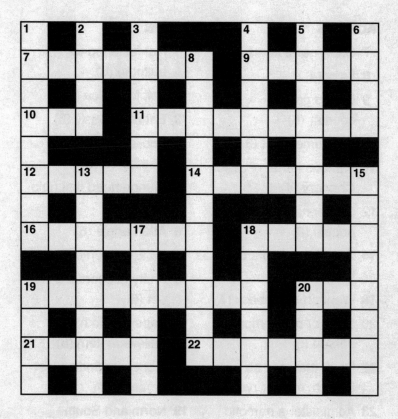

ACROSS

7 Short news items (8)

8 Lazy (4)

9 Dotted game counter (6)

10 Consume all of (3,2)

11 Famous father of Jason Connery (4)

12 Ginger-haired people (8)

14 Cosmetic used around the lashes (8)

18 Went on horseback (4)

20 Surly or bad-tempered person (5)

22 Drink that may be Scotch, malt or rye (6)

23 Administer a narcotic to (4)

24 Supply water to (land or crops) (8)

DOWN

1 Not fastened (of buttons) (6)

2 Left to choice (8)

3 Eat ravenously (6)

4 Published or distributed (6)

5 Plunge head first (into water) (4)

6 At an angle (6)

13 Salary, income (8)

15 Fruity dessert in a pot (6)

16 Paper or cloth tableware item (6)

17 Money for finding lost property (6)

19 North and South ___, US states (6)

21 Strong impulse (4)

ACROSS

7 Person performing dangerous feats in films (8)

8 Robin ___, outlaw of Sherwood forest (4)

9 Foot-propelled pleasure boat (6)

10 Form of industrial action in which work is delayed on purpose (2-4)

11 Happily picturesque (7)

13 Agreement to stop fighting (5)

15 Dirty look (5)

17 People selling their houses (7)

19 Grab away from (6)

21 Old pub (6)

23 ___ Moore, *Ghost* star (4)

24 Rubber-soled canvas shoe (8)

DOWN

1 Eye swelling (4)

2 Standing by, available for duty (2,4)

3 Chemical used in many cleaning agents (7)

4 Unforeseen obstacle (4)

5 Drink taken after another of a different kind (6)

6 Family vehicle (5,3)

12 Ornamental stoppered bottle for holding wines or spirits (8)

14 Sure that you are definitely correct (7)

16 ___ reach, easily accessible (6)

18 Invent, make (6)

20 Extravagant publicity (4)

22 Provoke, annoy (4)

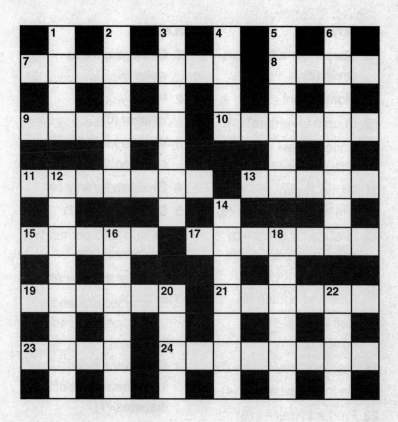

ACROSS

6 Shape like a flattened circle (7)

7 More recent (5)

9 People in general (4)

10 Boiled sweet with a sharp taste (4,4)

11 Dame Helen ___, UK film and TV actress (6)

13 First name shared by actresses Beckinsale and Winslet (4)

15 Kiss and cuddle (4)

16 Soft inner part of bones (6)

18 Single-storey house (8)

21 Be informed about (4)

22 Produce, deliver (5)

23 Reveal (information) (7)

DOWN

1 Damaging mass of water (5)

2 Preserving in vinegar (8)

3 World's largest continent (4)

4 Give temporarily (4)

5 Divert (traffic) (7)

8 Person who comes first in a contest (6)

12 Noise of thunder (6)

13 Boxing victory where your opponent can't get up (8)

14 Substance used in the treatment of diabetes (7)

17 Dance involving a line of people (5)

19 Common seabird (4)

20 Hang around (4)

ACROSS

1 Unwanted consequence (of a drug) (4,6)

8 Myth or moral story (5)

9 Schoolgirls' game (7)

10 Feeling of worry and apprehension (7)

11 Not a soul (2-3)

12 Large-winged insect (9)

15 Beat of blood in the wrist (5)

17 Off your guard (7)

19 Italian meat-filled pasta dish (7)

20 Habitual practice (5)

21 Indulged in idle fantasy (10)

DOWN

2 Place for newly arrived emails (5)

3 Examination at the optician's (3,4)

4 Strange rather than amusing (5,8)

5 ___ John, singer (5)

6 Cover to keep your brew warm (3,4)

7 Fact used by a detective (4)

8 Young horse (4)

12 Dear to the heart (7)

13 Mathematical equation (7)

14 Variety, sort (4)

15 Sound associated with a contented cat (4)

16 Extremely hard dark wood (5)

18 Astonish, surprise (5)

ACROSS

1 School topic (English, eg) (7)
5 Happening (5)
9 Stirred up and added coal to (a fire or furnace) (6)
10 Spice that goes well with egg custards (6)
11 Short and fat (5)
12 Germ-free or infertile (7)
14 ___ fan, device used to remove kitchen fumes (9)
18 Ask for advice or information from (7)
20 Break out of an egg (5)
22 Wayne Rooney's wife (6)
23 Think of, consider (6)
24 ___ West, hip-hop musician (5)
25 Coastal area (7)

DOWN

2 Incorrect, false (6)
3 Record-playing machine (7)
4 *The Da Vinci* ___, Dan Brown blockbuster (4)
6 One of the electorate (5)
7 Embroiderer's tool (6)
8 Come ___, break down (7)
13 Lengthen (7)
15 Citrus fruits (7)
16 Capital city of Colombia (6)
17 Frightened (6)
19 Shabby, sleazy (5)
21 Plant with a trunk (4)

ACROSS

1 ___ Forsyth, TV entertainer (5)
4 Goblin, dwarf (5)
9 Design for the first time (6)
10 Paper picture (6)
12 Reprimand fiercely (4,1,5,3)
13 Everlasting (7)
18 Costly but useless possession (5,8)
19 Yet, all the same (4,2)
20 Small hut for a dog (6)
21 Boggy land (5)
22 Andrew ___ Webber, *Cats* composer (5)

DOWN

2 Expose, show (6)
3 Substitute for glasses (7,6)
5 Supermodel born in Streatham in 1970 (5,8)
6 Means, way (6)
7 Number of seconds in a minute (5)
8 Small farm in Scotland (5)
11 Frighten suddenly (7)
14 Sugary (5)
15 The flicks! (6)
16 Delicately neat (6)
17 Market pitch (5)

ACROSS

3 Small amount (3)

7 Zodiac sign of the Twins (6)

8 Rascally, wickedly playful (6)

9 Group of actors who work together (6)

10 Ransacker, thief (6)

11 Food delivery service for the elderly (5,2,6)

13 (Learn) by rote, without thought (6-7)

18 Crackling sound on the radio (6)

19 Caution with money (6)

20 Balloon gas (6)

21 Governing (6)

22 Big ___, London clock tower (3)

DOWN

1 Unit used when measuring temperature (6)

2 Ceremonial custom (6)

3 Search with a ___, check very thoroughly (4-5,4)

4 Popular blue-and-white pottery design (6,7)

5 Be against (6)

6 In addition (2,4)

11 Diagram in an atlas (3)

12 Morally wicked act (3)

14 Deer's horn (6)

15 Economic sector concerning shops (6)

16 Scarcely, only just (6)

17 Insult, outrage (6)

ACROSS

5 Re-equip (a room) (9)

8 Quiet lane (6)

9 School exam, usually at the age of 17-18 (1,5)

10 Chunk of wood (3)

11 Brief, revealing (of clothing) (6)

13 Without difficulty (6)

15 Person who makes a living from the land (6)

18 Snag, drawback (6)

20 ___ Mendes, Cuban-American actress (3)

21 Fastest pace of a horse (6)

22 Getting up (6)

23 Chemical substances in food (9)

DOWN

1 Improve, make more effective (6)

2 Pleasant to hug (6)

3 Infuriate, madden (6)

4 Estimate the value of (6)

6 Horse-riding events (9)

7 Standing or filling in for (9)

12 Closed pastry-case (3)

14 Feel poorly (3)

16 Tune, song (6)

17 Fix, mend (6)

18 Small, strong, onion-like bulb (6)

19 Part of a shoe (6)

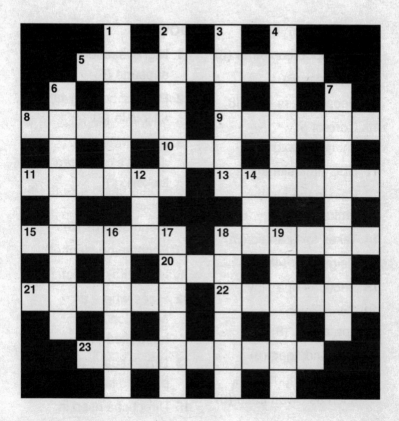

ACROSS

7 Shampoo container (6)

8 In tatters (6)

9 Became less wide (8)

10 Correct or improve (text) (4)

11 BBC time signal (4)

12 Pain in the lumbar region (8)

14 Takes for granted (8)

16 Reign over (4)

18 Sections of a play (4)

20 Concerning operations (8)

22 Over-indulged (6)

23 Dance performance, such as *Swan Lake* (6)

DOWN

1 Highly seasoned Italian sausage (6)

2 Parts of songs where all join in (8)

3 Pack away (in an aircraft's overhead locker) (4)

4 Makes, manufactures (8)

5 Frightening giant (4)

6 Unhealthy fixation (6)

12 Place where an explosion has happened (4,4)

13 Green space for a plane to land (8)

15 Directions used in cooking (6)

17 Person in charge (6)

19 Mix (ingredients) with a spoon (4)

21 Red precious stone (4)

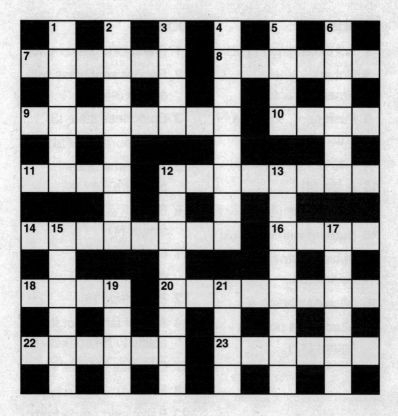

ACROSS

7 Act of barging in (12)

8 Robert ___ Jr, American actor (6)

9 Push hard, squeeze or crush (5)

10 Cagey behaviour (8)

13 A few (4)

15 Be anxious (4)

16 Burning with water (8)

17 Vehicle's steering device (5)

19 Allowed portion (6)

21 Murders (a political figure) (12)

DOWN

1 Prehistoric creature (8)

2 Render senseless with a blow (4)

3 Colourless state (8)

4 Clever one-liner (4)

5 Tense and under pressure (8)

6 Diana ___, Motown singer (4)

11 Forming an obstacle (2,3,3)

12 Esplanade (8)

14 Animal famed for its ability to kill snakes (8)

17 Opposite of 'east' (4)

18 Final (4)

20 Ballet skirt made from many layers of net (4)

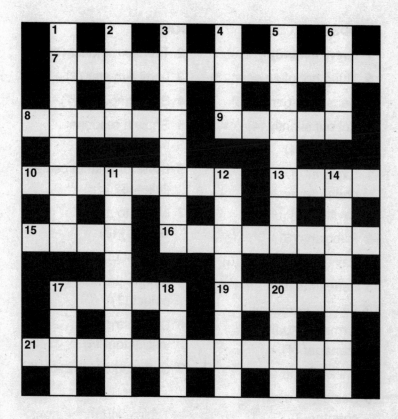

ACROSS

1 Every time (6)

5 Thing not often seen (6)

8 Causes of germs (8)

9 Act out silently (4)

10 Leg joint (4)

11 Explorer of underground cavities (8)

12 Rubbishy (6)

13 Painful experience (6)

15 Pedestrianised area (8)

18 Sir ___ Ferguson, former football manager (4)

19 Wicked, bad (4)

20 Settle in a new country (8)

21 Wanting to have a baby (6)

22 Simple but cosy (6)

DOWN

2 Trainee motorist (7,6)

3 Lady film star (7)

4 Bad-tempered (7)

5 Show a response, behave (5)

6 Lover of Shakespeare's Juliet (5)

7 Liable to mood swings (13)

13 Largest of all birds (7)

14 Simple drawing of an object (7)

16 Large stringed instrument (5)

17 Suffering deprivation (5)

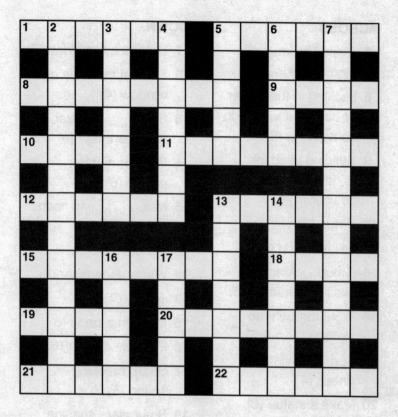

ACROSS

7 Animal lacking skin pigmentation (6)

8 Lacking in the power or competence (to do something) (6)

9 Building used for grinding grain into powder (4)

10 Virtue (8)

11 Tell apart (11)

14 Group looking for a missing person (6,5)

18 Right through the alphabet (4,1,2,1)

19 Common winter illness (4)

20 Make a statue (6)

21 Prepare for exams (6)

DOWN

1 Unlawful, forbidden (7)

2 Shelf at the base of a window (4)

3 Steve ___, creator of Alan Partridge (6)

4 Popular number puzzle (6)

5 Milk of ___, stomach medicine (8)

6 School form (5)

12 Warm underwear (8)

13 Trendy (7)

15 Move in a circle (6)

16 Possible danger (6)

17 Sharp breaking sound (5)

19 Smugglers' seaside hideaway (4)

ACROSS

7 Woman formerly employed to wait at table (11)

8 District (6)

9 Swindler (3,3)

10 Rootless wanderers (8)

11 Travel by horse (4)

12 Image of a god (4)

14 Standard pattern (8)

17 Expensive wool (6)

19 Keanu ___, star of 1999's *The Matrix* (6)

20 Period of fifty years (4-7)

DOWN

1 Come into sight (6)

2 Productive, profitable (8)

3 ___ Barker, *Porridge* actor (6)

4 Spring-blooming plant with white, yellow or purple flowers (6)

5 Young deer (4)

6 Prince ___, Earl of Wessex (6)

11 Arrived (6,2)

13 Small inflatable boat (6)

14 Hypnotic state resembling sleep (6)

15 Soldier trained to fight on both land and sea (6)

16 Method of producing textile patterns (3-3)

18 ___ Murs, *Dance with Me Tonight* singer (4)

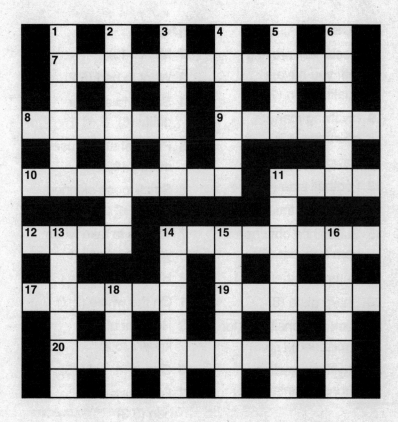

ACROSS

1 Document proving that you have a qualification (11)
9 Involving many countries (13)
10 Dawdled (8)
12 Football side (4)
14 One more time (5)
15 Substance obtained from tree sap (5)
19 Camper's shelter (4)
20 Sharp taste (8)
22 Took responsibility (for a misdeed) (7,3,3)
24 Physical exertion, during cleaning (5,6)

DOWN

2 Munch (3)
3 Went to bed (6,2)
4 Set up to appear guilty (6)
5 Piece of metal, used as money (4)
6 Small loose-skinned variety of orange (9)
7 Tablets to take when you are unwell (5)
8 Hold responsible (5)
11 On the whole (2,7)
13 How should I know? (6,2)
16 Goods for sale (5)
17 Frankfurter in a bun (3,3)
18 Consuming (5)
21 Chauffeur-driven car, for short (4)
23 Crispy lettuce (3)

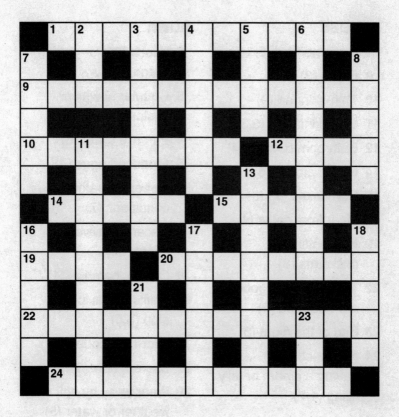

ACROSS

1 Crammed full (5-1-5)
9 Finish (3)
10 Thin-skinned (9)
11 Loaf container (5,3)
12 Bathroom powder (4)
14 Niche, alcove (6)
16 Cornflakes, eg (6)
18 Meat from cattle (4)
19 Non-batting cricketers (8)
22 Trading where goods are swapped (9)
23 Bird of the night (3)
24 (Of chocolates) having a cream or jelly filling (4-7)

DOWN

2 Bushy field or garden barrier (5)
3 Counter at which customers pay (4,4)
4 Parent's sister (6)
5 Produced eggs (4)
6 General weather conditions (7)
7 Recently delivered infant (7,4)
8 Cruelly, harshly (11)
13 Traffic signal to stop (3,5)
15 Informal goodbye (7)
17 Sacred, holy (6)
20 Wear away by action of weather or water (5)
21 Payment to a landlord (4)

ACROSS

1 Show off, brag (5)

4 Update (of a licence, eg) (7)

8 Pedestrian route (7)

9 Fillet or T-bone, eg (5)

10 ___ Portman, Oscar-winning actress (7)

12 Noisy fight (5)

14 Rendering unconscious (8,3)

18 Hard to climb (5)

19 Sale inviting bids (7)

21 Person now living and working abroad (5)

23 Book section title (7)

24 Person who stalks at night (7)

25 First name of actress Ms Arterton (5)

DOWN

1 Greeting formally (6)

2 Suddenly and without warning (3,2,4)

3 Absorbent cloth (5)

4 Beam of sunlight (3)

5 Feeder for a horse (7)

6 Word meaning 'small' in Scotland (3)

7 *The ___ Lads*, old sitcom (6)

11 Lloyd Webber/Rice stage and screen musical (5)

13 Silvery-white metal (9)

15 Country's chief city (7)

16 Kipping (6)

17 Baffling riddle (6)

20 Daniel ___, James Bond actor (5)

22 Go to the next page (inits)(3)

23 Belonging to that woman (3)

ACROSS

1 Small towers (7)

5 Loud noise made by a lion (4)

10 Father (3)

11 Poverty (9)

12 ___ Martin, lead singer of Coldplay (5)

13 Feeling of being worried, sad or shocked (6)

15 Crushes (grapes) with the feet (6)

17 Instinctive movement (6)

18 One-room accommodation (6)

20 Underwater swimmer (5)

23 Separation, remoteness (9)

24 Precious stone (3)

25 Turn sharply (4)

26 ___ home, large house often open to tourists (7)

DOWN

2 Beneath, directly below (5)

3 Position next to the scene of action (8,4)

4 Fashion, mode (5)

6 Worker's garment (7)

7 Hazard (4)

8 School, instruct (7)

9 Actress in *Spider-Man* (7,5)

14 Excessive, way beyond the norm (7)

16 Very ugly building (7)

19 Swivel (5)

21 Long watch at night (5)

22 Chicken ___, poultry dish (4)

ACROSS

1 Narrow-brimmed hat with a dented crown (6)

4 Characterised by unusual traits (6)

9 ___ Baba, *Arabian Nights* character (3)

10 Large group of classical musicians (9)

11 Played a role (5)

12 Describe clearly (7)

14 Taking part in a risky activity (11)

17 Surname of former Bond star Pierce (7)

18 Person in competition with another (5)

20 Arrest for a crime (9)

22 Uncle ___, USA's nickname (3)

23 Official messenger, in the past (6)

24 Close at hand (6)

DOWN

1 Cuppa-making sachet (3,3)

2 Silly twit (5)

3 Large flat pea-like vegetable (5,4)

5 Put to some purpose (3)

6 Learn new skills (7)

7 Long (for) (5)

8 Replies to party invitations (11)

13 Bird related to the pheasant and grouse (9)

15 Instrument for administering small amounts of liquid (7)

16 Awkward, ungainly (6)

17 Sandy place by the sea (5)

19 Cap's shade against the sun (5)

21 Conger ___, fish (3)

ACROSS

8 Letter at the beginning of a word (7)

9 Prolonged stay in bed in the morning (3-2)

10 Sailing vessel (5)

11 Captivate, bewitch (7)

12 Time when most people take holidays (6,6)

16 Grovel, apologise (3,6,3)

20 Store selling balls, dolls and games (3,4)

23 Lift with difficulty (5)

24 Ready and willing (5)

25 Christmas chocolate cake (4,3)

DOWN

1 Common plastic material (5)

2 Make an error of addition (8)

3 One who is injured in a crime or accident (6)

4 French word for 'she' (4)

5 Overused phrase (6)

6 Greek cheese (4)

7 Precise moment in time (7)

13 Bone attached to the backbone (3)

14 Aptly, fittingly (8)

15 Material made from animal skin (7)

17 Free from injury (6)

18 Breathe out (6)

19 Occupy the throne (5)

21 Form of meditation and exercise (4)

22 Settles an account (4)

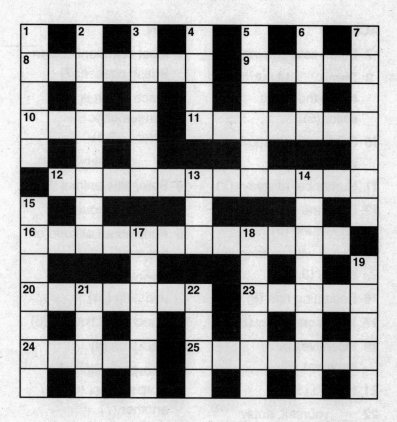

ACROSS

7 Small-time criminal (7)

9 Dame ___ MacArthur, round-the-world sailor (5)

10 Continuous humming sound (5)

11 Numerical (display) (7)

12 Up in the ___, still undecided (3)

13 Graph with rectangular blocks (3,5)

16 Becoming ripe (8)

17 Waste container (3)

19 Incentives or impulses (7)

21 Not old (5)

22 ___ yourself, apply effort (5)

23 Father's father (7)

DOWN

1 Most commonly eaten British cheese (7)

2 Place which is dangerous to enter (2-2,4)

3 Or ___, otherwise (4)

4 Spiky little animal (8)

5 Surplus amount (4)

6 Adopted an attitude of prayer (5)

8 Renovating, updating (11)

13 Bunches of flowers (8)

14 Backfires (8)

15 Reorganisation of a word's letters to form another (7)

18 Lopsided, wonky (5)

20 Topped, as a cake (4)

21 Twelve-month period (4)

ACROSS

7 Paradise (6)

8 Stay, be left (6)

10 Pair of entertainers (6,3)

11 First name of actress Ms Basinger (3)

12 Time after which TV programmes unsuitable for children are shown (9)

14 Zero score in football, for instance (3)

15 ___ and Tina Turner, 1960s pop duo (3)

16 Provided financial support to (9)

18 Gloomy (3)

20 Harass, hunt down (9)

21 One of two instruments crashed together (6)

22 Place housing historic items (6)

DOWN

1 Darkness out of the sun (6)

2 Long French stick of bread (8)

3 Announces openly or formally (8)

4 Encounter (4)

5 Face-covering (4)

6 Creature (6)

9 Instrument panel in a car (9)

13 Served (food) (6,2)

14 Cherished, cared for (8)

15 Creepy-crawly (6)

17 Saw in your sleep (6)

19 Blast! (4)

20 Ring of bells (4)

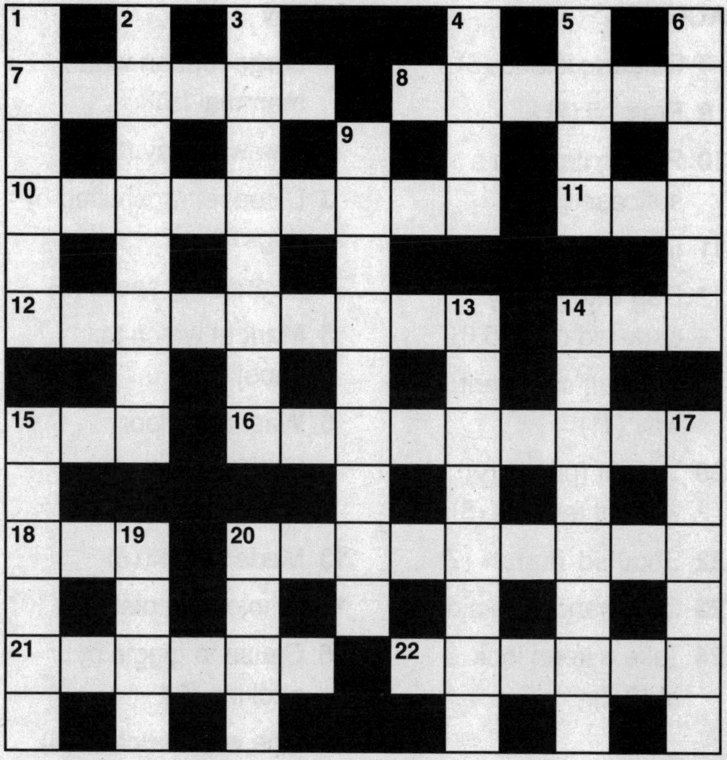

ACROSS

8 Balearic island (5)

9 Pretend (7)

10 Putting items in a suitcase (7)

11 Income before tax (5)

12 Dog with a silky dark-red coat (5,6)

14 In a self-confident way (11)

20 Vacant (property), without tenants (5)

22 Shouted 'hurrah' (7)

23 Command, direction (7)

24 Take a keen look at (3,2)

DOWN

1 Large African water mammal (5)

2 Throws away (8)

3 Disease transmitted by dogs (6)

4 Overeating spells (6)

5 Mark at which to shoot (6)

6 Washable floor covering (4)

7 Muddled, untidy (5)

13 Made bigger (8)

15 Whole, complete (6)

16 Cause to giggle by stroking (6)

17 One who watches (6)

18 Second meal of the day, usually (5)

19 Change to fit the environment (5)

21 Queue (4)

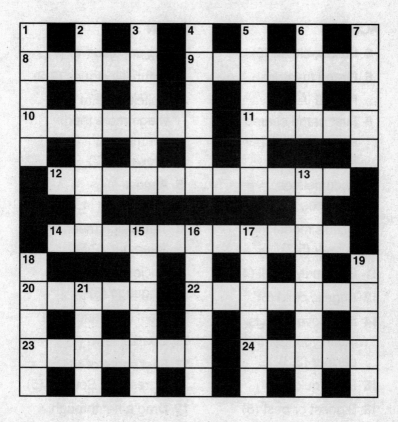

ACROSS

1 Follow, chase (6)

5 Grand theatrical ending (6)

8 First name shared by actresses Hatcher and Polo (4)

9 Accumulates, amasses (8)

10 Child's model railway (5,3)

11 Extremely small (4)

12 Angelic child (6)

14 Male lover who is much younger than his partner (3,3)

16 Read quickly (4)

18 Biggest or best (8)

20 Comedian and TV presenter (4,4)

21 Grew old (4)

22 TV or video control device (6)

23 Arthur ___, US playwright and third husband of Marilyn Monroe (6)

DOWN

2 Dig up, discover (7)

3 Futuristic stories (3-2)

4 Suitcases that weigh more than the maximum limit allowed (6,7)

5 Almost overflowing (4,2,3,4)

6 Traffic sign meaning 'keep out' (2,5)

7 Ancient Roman language (5)

13 Meet by chance (3,4)

15 Coarse, lewd (7)

17 First name of US actress Ms Sevigny (5)

19 Drag a net through water (5)

06 Growing sign of a
cut (7)

20 Returns the ball,
when it touches the
ground (7)

24 Smallest barrel (5)

46 meets a
meantime? (9)

20 Bela's hand (9)

ACROSS

1 Squander (5)
4 If really necessary (2,1,4)
9 Cutlery item for stirring a drink (8)
10 Pleasure excursion (4)
11 Single thread (6)
12 Small bay, creek (5)
13 Be sullen (4)
15 Bite or pinch (3)
16 Boo (4)
17 South American woolly pack animal (5)
19 Covered walk with shops (6)
21 Comfy (4)
22 Showing signs of a cold (8)
23 Returns the ball before it touches the ground (7)
24 Smallest banknote (5)

DOWN

2 Prevent, ward off (5)
3 Left over, extra (2,5)
5 Sportsperson having a game of singles or doubles (6,6)
6 Colourful part of a flower head (5)
7 Wooden pin knocked down with a ball (7)
8 Notoriously quick-tempered TV chef (6,6)
14 Popular resort city in Florida (7)
16 Bath with underwater jets (7)
18 Heavenly messenger (5)
20 School nitwit (5)

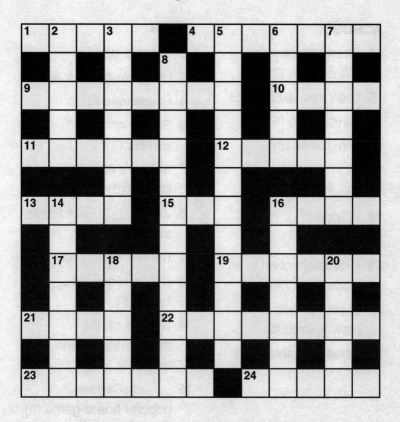

ACROSS

1 Strong emotion or enthusiasm (7)
5 Look into, explore (5)
9 Film, movie (6,7)
10 Army units (8)
11 Cram for exams (4)
12 Usually, normally (9)
16 Wagon (4)
17 Thugs (8)
19 Industrial action in all industries (7,6)
21 Jester, or wild playing-card (5)
22 Acrobatic athlete (7)

DOWN

2 On ship (6)
3 Fairground see-saw (9)
4 Possessed (5)
6 Furrow made by wheels (3)
7 Animal's hole in the ground (6)
8 Jackie ___, *Reet Petite* singer (6)
11 Continue doggedly (7,2)
13 Kilt's chequered fabric (6)
14 Survive on the inadequate means available (4,2)
15 ___ and ladders, popular board-game (6)
18 Pernickety (5)
20 Woolly farm female (3)

ACROSS

1 Player of a Scottish wind instrument (8)

6 Band worn over the shoulder (4)

8 Type of crossword clue (6)

9 Put in order, tidy (6)

10 Builder's hard-setting floor substance (8)

13 Small lake (4)

14 Places to hang headwear (9)

17 Fish's breathing organ (4)

18 Diluted drinks (8)

19 Slum district (6)

21 Cause to fall (6)

23 Factual (4)

24 US singer whose real name is Stefani Joanne Angelina Germanotta (4,4)

DOWN

2 Weight for holding a ship steady (6)

3 Non-amateur (3)

4 Has, owns (9)

5 Move fast (3)

6 Sudden rushes of animals in panic (9)

7 Perceiving with the eyes (6)

11 ___ Brontë, author of *Jane Eyre* (9)

12 Calculated the worth of (9)

15 Further up (6)

16 Aeroplane-induced tiredness due to time differences (3,3)

20 Substance obtained from olives (3)

22 Small short-haired dog with a wrinkled face (3)

ACROSS

1 Man or boy (4)
4 Citadel, stronghold (8)
8 Finger-shaped cream cake (6)
9 Spinach-eating cartoon sailor (6)
10 Stone granules (4)
11 Fair shares for all (8)
13 Removal from an electricity supply (13)
16 Sloped (8)
19 Opposite of west (4)
20 Girl from abroad who acts as babysitter in exchange for board and lodging (2,4)
22 Determined, purposeful (6)
23 Artist's pigment jar (5,3)
24 Start of nightfall (4)

DOWN

2 Squeezed instrument with a keyboard (9)
3 Stretchy material (7)
4 Comedy play (5)
5 Break or burst (7)
6 Drive off, push back (5)
7 Upper atmosphere (3)
12 Hundreds and ___, cake decorations (9)
14 Less messy (gloss or emulsion) (3-4)
15 Gave medical care to (7)
17 Commit (facts) to memory (5)
18 Float aimlessly (5)
21 American film actress Miss Thurman (3)

ACROSS

1 (Had) ripped (4)

4 Boarded a ship (8)

8 (Of the night sky) twinkly (6)

9 Brilliant brain (6)

10 Bean used as a meat substitute (4)

11 Worn to shreds (8)

13 In a self-reliant way (13)

16 Breaking out of jail (8)

19 Become weary (4)

20 Garbage (6)

22 Starting point (6)

23 Copies, mimics (8)

24 *Radio* ___, Queen song (2,2)

DOWN

2 Money spent (9)

3 Provide a commentary (7)

4 Country famous for its Pyramids, capital Cairo (5)

5 Unshakeably prejudiced (7)

6 Wash in clear water (5)

7 Ostrich-like bird (3)

12 Making (photographs) bigger (9)

14 Obvious, clear (7)

15 Zero, nought (7)

17 Over the age of eighteen (5)

18 Shiny finish (5)

21 Rough-leaved tall tree (3)

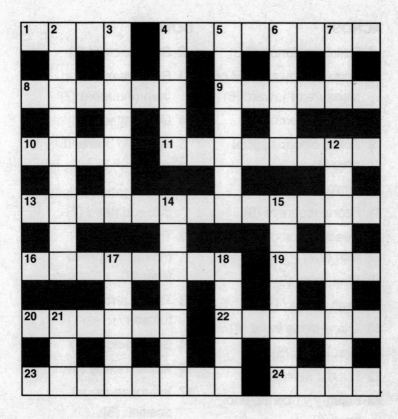

ACROSS

1 Ballroom dance (3-3)

5 Persuade by an offer of pleasure or reward (6)

8 Ghastly, horrible (8)

9 Police officer's patrol area (4)

10 Lower jaw (4)

11 Fearless, brave (8)

12 Reach a compromise with (4,7)

15 Shut away (8)

18 Swift attack (4)

20 Three-piece band (4)

21 First letters (8)

22 Filled a suitcase (6)

23 Flash ___, comic-book hero (6)

DOWN

2 Severe, cruel (5)

3 Remove make-up from (the face) (7)

4 Do away with (7)

5 Vote into power (5)

6 Piece of furniture (5)

7 Organisation helping those in need (7)

12 Tropical mosquito-spread fever (7)

13 Taking a room in a house (7)

14 Brave soldier (7)

16 Appal, horrify (5)

17 In bronze medal position (5)

19 House made of ice (5)

ACROSS

7 Living in water (7)

9 Have words, bicker (5)

10 Fairy-like creature (3)

11 Family under one roof (9)

12 Sleepy (5)

14 Readiness to face and endure danger (7)

16 Proposer of fundamental reforms (7)

18 Add together, calculate (3,2)

19 Outrageous or hideous (9)

20 Glass container (3)

21 Flavour (5)

22 Spend a lot of money (7)

DOWN

1 Animal that devours people (3-5)

2 Wide stretch of water (4)

3 Designed on metal (6)

4 Rich creamy layered cake (6)

5 Uncouth through lack of knowledge (8)

6 Look after (plants) (4)

8 Local politicians (11)

13 Lack of manners (8)

15 Person shipping goods to the continent (8)

17 Small (lamb) chop (6)

18 Rough-and-tumble struggle (6)

19 Baseball glove (4)

20 Panel of twelve people in court (4)

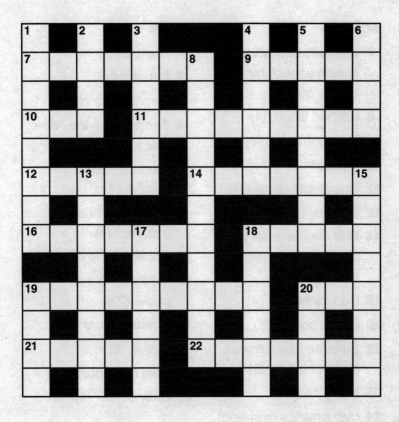

ACROSS

7 Man with two wives or woman with two husbands (8)

8 Kitchen fixture (4)

9 TV commercial (6)

10 Opposite of 'mine' (5)

11 Newcastle's river (4)

12 Weirdos (8)

14 Mull over in order to make an informed decision (8)

18 Den, hideaway (4)

20 Snake poison (5)

22 Surprise attack from a place of hiding (6)

23 Nought (4)

24 Mathematics of shape etc (8)

DOWN

1 Noon (6)

2 Ditherers (8)

3 French-style cafe (6)

4 Remained in the same place (6)

5 Hindu spiritual teacher (4)

6 Glittering Christmas streamer (6)

13 Spoke off the cuff (2-6)

15 Exhibited to the public (2,4)

16 Physical harm (6)

17 Motive (6)

19 Take out a policy (6)

21 Cosy corner (4)

ACROSS

7 Hardens, becomes rigid (8)

8 Fluffy material on a sticking plaster (4)

9 Most strange (6)

10 Investigator (6)

11 Thing given as a gift (7)

13 Wander off course (5)

15 Courtroom boss (5)

17 Ambushes, accosts (7)

19 Mollycoddle (6)

21 Houses of Parliament clock tower (3,3)

23 Playwright Bennett's first name (4)

24 Garden tree with attractive flowers (8)

DOWN

1 Small simple earring (4)

2 Course following the main one at a meal (6)

3 Trying, experimenting (7)

4 Invites (to a party) (4)

5 Able to speak a language with ease (6)

6 Rickety (8)

12 Fit for recycling (8)

14 Household waste (7)

16 Wide open, yawning (6)

18 Shallow body of salt water linked to the sea (6)

20 Italy's capital (4)

22 Way out (4)

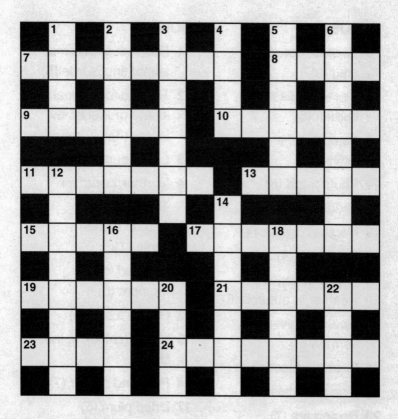

ACROSS

6 Twisted, out of shape (7)

7 Desert's beast of burden (5)

9 As dead as a ___, extinct (4)

10 Photograph (8)

11 Images in sleep (6)

13 Magician's stick (4)

15 One thing (4)

16 ___ summer, warm weather in autumn (6)

18 One who gives a sermon (8)

21 Involving bloodshed (4)

22 Fine porcelain (5)

23 Raging fire (7)

DOWN

1 Fact that shows that something is true (5)

2 Three-dimensional image produced by lasers (8)

3 Lock openers (4)

4 Northern word for 'girl' (4)

5 Add up (votes) again (7)

8 Stopped for a moment (6)

12 Get off a bus (6)

13 Herds (cattle), in the US (8)

14 Prim and proper (7)

17 Dried plum (5)

19 Teenage skin complaint (4)

20 Chimed (4)

ACROSS

1 Footwear cleaner (4,6)

8 Lighter in colour (5)

9 Part of the body which can sometimes be ingrowing (7)

10 Former, previous (3-4)

11 Metric petrol unit (5)

12 In a fit condition to fly (9)

15 Stage trickery (5)

17 Shake from fear or cold (7)

19 Dried fruit (7)

20 ___ Fox, US actress and model (5)

21 Sugary fairground treat (10)

DOWN

2 Divide into two equal parts (5)

3 Before now (7)

4 Quite the opposite (2,3,8)

5 Absolutely perfect (5)

6 In good physical condition (7)

7 Sticky substance used as an adhesive (4)

8 Game like snooker (4)

12 Sweet and innocent (7)

13 Variety of underwear that keeps you extra-warm (7)

14 Person older than twelve but younger than twenty (4)

15 Roman Catholic service (4)

16 Series of metal links (5)

18 Phoney, sham (5)

ACROSS

1 Jennifer ___, Hollywood actress and *Friends* star (7)
5 Advantage or property (5)
9 In a state of inactivity (2,4)
10 Sent by post (6)
11 Subject or theme of a book or speech (5)
12 Said, spoke (7)
14 Fruit popular in a muffin (9)
18 International singing star whose songs include *Vogue* (7)
20 County south of Suffolk (5)
22 Book of accounts (6)
23 Pester, irritate (6)
24 Main part of a tree (5)
25 Half of 140 (7)

DOWN

2 People of a particular country (6)
3 Distinctive, unusual (7)
4 Solemn undertaking to tell the truth (4)
6 Take forcibly (5)
7 Small hole in a shoe for a lace (6)
8 Ever so many (7)
13 St ___, mountain-rescue dog (7)
15 Showjumping winner's badge of ribbon (7)
16 Course of a working life (6)
17 Warm up (food, eg) again (6)
19 Instrument with keyboard and pipes (5)
21 Skilled and talented (4)

ACROSS

1 Extremely angry (5)
4 Opponent in a battle (5)
9 Item delivered by a postal worker (6)
10 Record or CD player with two speakers (6)
12 Actor in the title role of *Batman Begins* (9,4)
13 Boil or bake in advance (7)
18 Chain of peaks (8,5)
19 Small computer (6)
20 Spot, zit (6)
21 Round flat hat (5)
22 Drink similar in taste to cider (5)

DOWN

2 Give up work because of advancing age (6)
3 Hidden store of delightful things (8,5)
5 No way! (3,2,4,4)
6 ___ Carey, US singer (6)
7 Pull out (hairs) (5)
8 Bee's produce (5)
11 Lap of a racing track (7)
14 Odour, scent (5)
15 Dark mauve (6)
16 Concealed rifleman (6)
17 Turn for information (to) (5)

ACROSS

3 Divide into pieces with a knife (3)

7 Man's jacket (6)

8 Sloping style of writing (6)

9 Buzz off! (4,2)

10 Game played on grass, clay or hard courts (6)

11 Government employee (6,7)

13 Outstrip, be much better than (5,8)

18 Complete failure (6)

19 Words of wisdom (6)

20 Fact that others are not meant to know (6)

21 Damned or swore (6)

22 That woman (3)

DOWN

1 Writing-table with drawers (6)

2 Concerning teeth (6)

3 Games involving physical rough and tumble (7,6)

4 Favour one side and precipitate an action (3,3,7)

5 In-car system that directs drivers (6)

6 Ability to see (6)

11 Chum, mate (3)

12 Strip of paper used as a label (3)

14 Departed (6)

15 Dressing room in a church (6)

16 Reroute (6)

17 American slang for five cents (6)

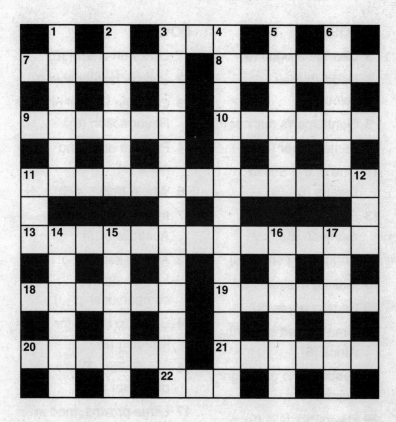

17 Crew members tried with bread, unbeaten!

18 Nouns and (11)

19 New voyager an old guitar (6)

ACROSS

5 Change around (9)
8 Reddish (hair colour) (6)
9 Gentleman's outfitter (6)
10 Female deer (3)
11 One of the Seven Dwarfs (6)
13 Ruler in place of a monarch (6)
15 Annual dog show (6)
18 Making mistakes (6)
20 English apple (3)
21 Great desert of North Africa (6)
22 Tendency to get angry quickly (6)
23 Hikers' holdalls (9)

DOWN

1 Lure with charm (6)
2 Stylish, fashionable (6)
3 Christian festival of the Resurrection (6)
4 Process of getting older (6)
6 Whole (milk) (4-5)
7 Informal name for Australia (4,5)
12 Animal kept for pleasure or companionship (3)
14 Body part used for listening (3)
16 ___ Cotton, TV presenter (6)
17 Large prawns, fried in breadcrumbs (6)
18 Add-ons (6)
19 New version of an old film (6)

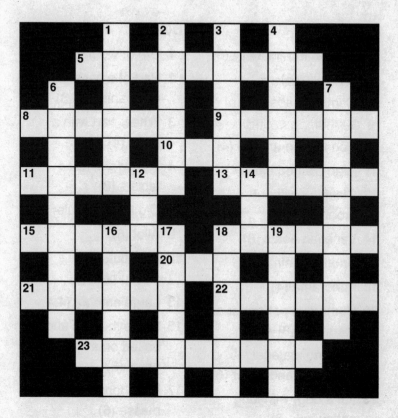

ACROSS

7 Happening annually (6)

8 Aid, help (6)

9 Complete absence of light (8)

10 Rod to hold a towel (4)

11 High-pitched bark (4)

12 Claiming without proof (8)

14 Venetian boats (8)

16 Shout of pain (4)

18 Panorama (4)

20 Humorous performer on the stage (8)

22 Building material mixed with sand and water (6)

23 (Of a dog) with long untidy hair (6)

DOWN

1 Girl or woman (6)

2 Part of a car's stopping mechanism (5,3)

3 Wheel part with a tread (4)

4 Torpedo-shaped tablets (8)

5 Old Russian ruler (4)

6 Allot (6)

12 Distribute (resources) (8)

13 Large amount (4,4)

15 Stage musical and film based on a Dickens novel (6)

17 Rush forward en masse (6)

19 Cry (4)

21 Strong-smelling perfume ingredient (4)

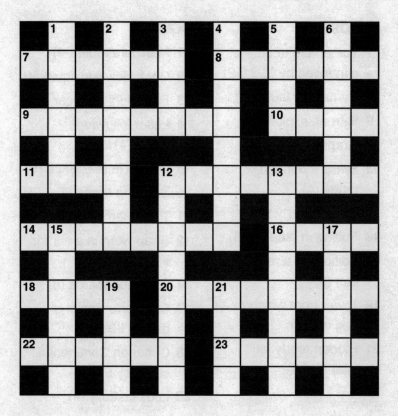

ACROSS

7 Vulnerable to or controlled by (2,3,5,2)

8 Damaged, faulty (6)

9 Ill-treat, exploit (5)

10 Graphs, charts (8)

13 Swiss mountain range (4)

15 Garden party (4)

16 Putting in (seeds) (8)

17 Edition (of a magazine etc) (5)

19 Tower from which peals ring out (6)

21 Hidden ready for later (2,4,6)

DOWN

1 Manicure tool (4-4)

2 Cook slowly in liquid (4)

3 Front light on a car (8)

4 Letter following alpha (4)

5 Person in residence (8)

6 Smelling organ (4)

11 Treat mercifully (2,4,2)

12 Strap worn in a car for safety (4,4)

14 Food cupboards (8)

17 Children's 'spotting' game (1-3)

18 Common Continental currency unit (4)

20 Look lustfully (4)

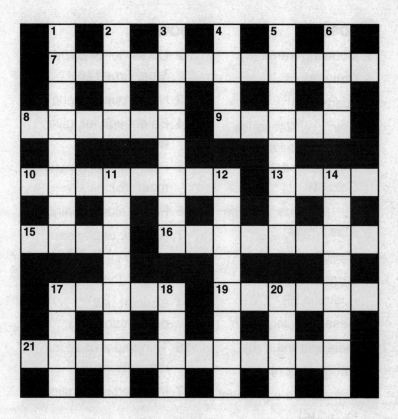

ACROSS

1 Counting frame (6)

5 Catty (6)

8 Judders (8)

9 *Star* ___, film series featuring Luke Skywalker and Han Solo (4)

10 ___ *the Blue*, Jessica Alba film (4)

11 Resign, retire (4,4)

12 Largest city in Australia (6)

13 Desert illusion (6)

15 Male astronaut (8)

18 Rough rock (4)

19 Female title equivalent to 'Sir' (4)

20 Alternative name for the German shepherd dog (8)

21 Upward climb (6)

22 Special natural ability (6)

DOWN

2 US singer of *Baby One More Time* (7,6)

3 Humorous drawing (7)

4 Be enough for, give enough to (7)

5 Pour fat over (roasting meat) (5)

6 Pulled along behind (5)

7 Another unpleasant repetition! (4,2,2,5)

13 Way of thinking (7)

14 Concert hall performance (7)

16 Thin paper used for decorations (5)

17 Intended or signified (5)

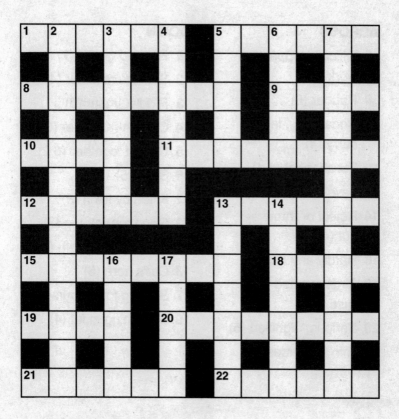

ACROSS

7 Official stoppage of work (6)

8 Rubber (6)

9 Rogan ___, lamb curry (4)

10 Fat chance! (4,4)

11 Level of hotness (11)

14 Reject or throw out (4,3,4)

18 Hardly any (3,2,3)

19 Birds reputed to be wise (4)

20 Serious, dignified (6)

21 Join the forces (6)

DOWN

1 Rubbed gently (7)

2 Satellite receiver (4)

3 Riddle, poser (6)

4 Curtain-rail cover (6)

5 Collect together (6,2)

6 Sobs (5)

12 Killed by toxin (8)

13 Good for nothing (7)

15 Increase in length (6)

16 Car's horn (6)

17 Sign up for a course (5)

19 Swimming in fat (4)

ACROSS

7 Process of breathing (11)

8 Shared the same view (6)

9 Place where lashes grow (6)

10 Arrogance (8)

11 Herb used as stuffing for poultry (4)

12 Move from side to side (4)

14 Theatrical outfits (8)

17 Political refuge (6)

19 Return or retreat (2,4)

20 In police custody (5,6)

DOWN

1 Mythical fire-breathing reptile (6)

2 Daily school meeting (8)

3 ___ East, Israel's region (6)

4 State in which you are free from danger (6)

5 Form of transport with pedals (4)

6 Finishing (6)

11 Slipped (8)

13 Clean dishes after a meal (4,2)

14 Film-maker's machine (6)

15 Sickly sweet (6)

16 Thrill, agitate (6)

18 Titled woman (4)

ACROSS

1 Temperature gauge (11)

9 In a state of suspense (2,11)

10 Kept for oneself (8)

12 Pentagon's number of sides (4)

14 Move stealthily along the ground (5)

15 Small American animal notorious for its smell (5)

19 Mark ___, member of Take That (4)

20 Glove thrown down as a challenge (8)

22 Not menacing (13)

24 Very important object or person in your life (5,3,3)

DOWN

2 Opposite of 'cold' (3)

3 Coated with plaster (8)

4 Unwrapped (a present) (6)

5 Sound which bounces back (4)

6 Expressing feelings (9)

7 Flower worn on Remembrance Sunday (5)

8 Posed a question (5)

11 Person who does woodwork (9)

13 Youth with cropped hair (8)

16 Of the tide, flow away from the shore (2,3)

17 Crescent-shaped fruit (6)

18 Part of a theatre (5)

21 Crossword pattern (4)

23 Groom's response (1,2)

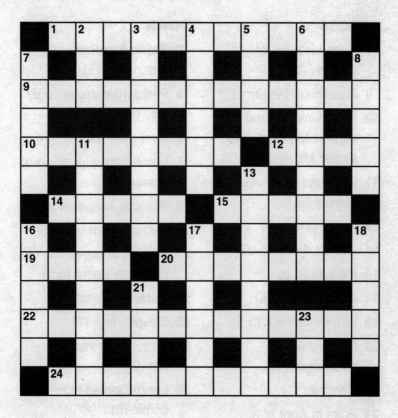

ACROSS

1 Term for a set of thirteen (6,5)
9 Getting on in years (3)
10 First name shared by actress Ms Ricci and singer Ms Aguilera (9)
11 Crowded and full of activity (8)
12 Notify (4)
14 One or the other (6)
16 Meddle (4,2)
18 Mob disorder (4)
19 Wooden shack (3,5)
22 Concealed passengers (9)
23 Chopper (3)
24 Point in front of a football goal where free shots are taken (7,4)

DOWN

2 South American mountains (5)
3 Performed exceedingly well (8)
4 Thin rope (6)
5 Force from a position of power (4)
6 Notable, respected (7)
7 Betray, stitch up (6-5)
8 Wicked or rebellious heavenly being (6,5)
13 Society's rejects (8)
15 Couple, pair (7)
17 Small open racing car (2-4)
20 Long-running kids' comic (5)
21 Hot rock from a volcano (4)

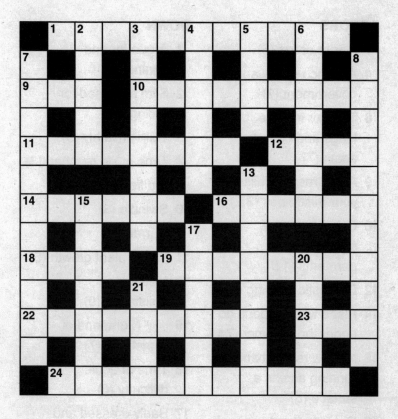

18 One who busts chattels
For hire (9)
21 Put out to candled (5)
23 Amount of room
Used in a single
Injection (5)
24 Stretched v,
26 Risky (5)

17 Body encased and no v
Do sea (6)
20 Equipped with
Weapons (8)
22 Alien spaces up tions)
(3)
24 Voting man (3)

ACROSS

1 Finger or toe (5)
4 Absence of law and government (7)
8 Take air into the lungs and blow it out again (7)
9 Admit responsibility for your misdoings (3,2)
10 Casual, usually short-sleeved, garments (1-6)
12 Domestic building (5)
14 Place where goods go under the hammer (7,4)
18 Narrow raised band running across a surface (5)
19 One who hunts animals for their fur (7)
21 Put out (a candle) (5)
23 Amount of money given in a single payment (4,3)
24 Alleviated (7)
25 Risky (5)

DOWN

1 Argue for and against (6)
2 Slim dog used for racing (9)
3 Train privately (5)
4 Time of life reached (3)
5 A different one (7)
6 Swindle (3)
7 Hurrah! (6)
11 Young plant growth (5)
13 Meeting no resistance (9)
15 ___ Night, end of Christmas (7)
16 Time of acute difficulty (6)
17 Badly dressed and dowdy (6)
20 Equipped with weapons (5)
22 Alien spaceship (inits) (3)
23 Young man (3)

ACROSS

1 Scolded (4,3)

5 Feel irritation of the skin (4)

10 Tierra ___ Fuego, isles near Cape Horn (3)

11 Parts of the body where the arms join the torso (9)

12 Do a sum (3,2)

13 Forgive, pardon (6)

15 Main element found in coal (6)

17 Official release of a new product (6)

18 US singer nicknamed 'Slim Shady' (6)

20 Take from your bank account (5)

23 Main church in a city (9)

24 Great wonder (3)

25 Roald ___, *Charlie and the Chocolate Factory* author (4)

26 Bacon variety (7)

DOWN

2 Gazed lasciviously at (5)

3 Upset the hopes of (12)

4 Turned to ice (5)

6 Betrayal of one's country (7)

7 One who entertains others as guests (4)

8 Go forward (7)

9 Covered in bruises (5,3,4)

14 ___ or not, in any case (7)

16 Second contest to decide the winner (7)

19 Excellence, worth (5)

21 Dummy bullet (5)

22 Chemical non-alkali (4)

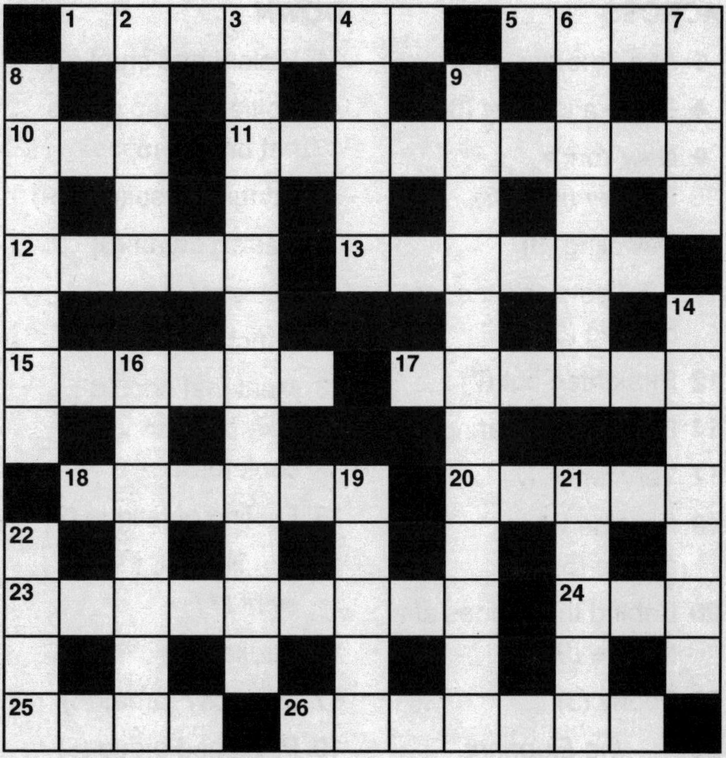
1
2
3
4
5
6
7
8
9
10
11
12
13
14
15
16
17
18
19
20
21
22
23
24
25
26

ACROSS

1 At a time previous to (6)
4 Begin a journey (3,3)
9 New York's country (inits) (3)
10 Dawdling (9)
11 Joint between the foot and leg (5)
12 Straighten out (7)
14 Bossy, overbearing (11)
17 Very tense (7)
18 Imagine while asleep (5)
20 Behind the scenes at a theatre (9)
22 Poorly (3)
23 ___ the Elephant, children's song (6)
24 Mount, climb (6)

DOWN

1 Violent and cruel (6)
2 Bottle to keep drinks hot or cold (5)
3 Bringing respite to (9)
5 Seeing organ (3)
6 Personal view (7)
7 Punch-up (5)
8 Meat that should take 60 seconds to cook (6,5)
13 Feeling of fatigue (9)
15 ___ illusion, trick of sight (7)
16 Strolled (6)
17 Inner-city (area) (5)
19 Privileged group (5)
21 Glide across snow (3)

ACROSS

8 Statement that shows you are sorry (7)

9 Selected (5)

10 ___ Foster, actress who won an Oscar for her role in *Silence of the Lambs* in 1991 (5)

11 Sudden fit (7)

12 Bricklayers' workplace (8,4)

16 Traditional, opposed to change (12)

20 Travelling amusement rides (7)

23 Twelfth of a year (5)

24 Large bird of prey (5)

25 Feel sure of the truth of (7)

DOWN

1 Round stringed instrument with a long neck (5)

2 Favour that deserves another (4,4)

3 Succeed, get on (2,4)

4 Holes in needles, or seed-buds in potatoes (4)

5 Performing in a play (6)

6 Versatile vegetarian foodstuff (4)

7 Removed (data) (7)

13 UK commercial broadcasting company (inits)(3)

14 Created (a new device) (8)

15 Scratched (shoes) (7)

17 Rubbed out (6)

18 Fall over (6)

19 Rudeness, disrespect (5)

21 ___ area, danger zone (2-2)

22 Judge's gown (4)

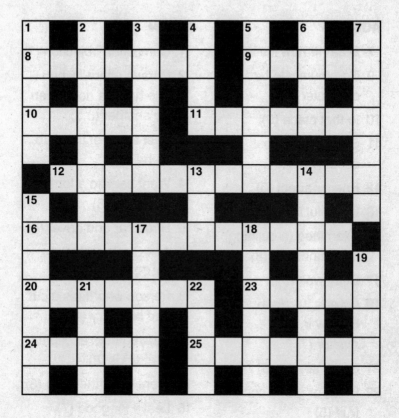

ACROSS

7 Breathe new life into (7)

9 Communicate by computer (5)

10 In that place (5)

11 Style of sloping script (7)

12 Enemy agent (3)

13 Dreadful incident (8)

16 Examined (a building) for soundness (8)

17 Baby wolf (3)

19 Gwen ___, Jean Harlow in _The Aviator_ (7)

21 Strict, severe (5)

22 Black or green cocktail fruit (5)

23 Bomb shot from a submarine (7)

DOWN

1 Complaint, objection (7)

2 Phrase uttered when one holds a door open for another (5,3)

3 Past tense of the verb 'to be' (4)

4 Went back to a former bad state (8)

5 Hired car and driver (4)

6 Ask God's protection for (5)

8 Person who does a cut and blow-dry (11)

13 Strayed from accepted standards (8)

14 Went over (the limit) (8)

15 Leave for good (7)

18 ___ Villa, Midlands soccer club (5)

20 Give out (radiation, eg) (4)

21 Traditional Hindu dress (4)

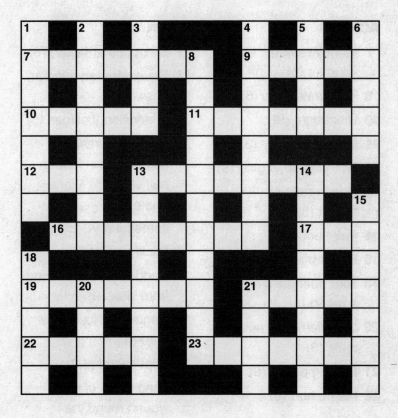

ACROSS

7 Money-saving voucher (6)

8 Terminate, stop (6)

10 Distraught (9)

11 Make a blunder (3)

12 Hurrying up, urging (9)

14 Dried grass as fodder (3)

15 Paint pot (3)

16 Had a trial run (9)

18 Tour operator's agent in a resort (3)

20 Qualities of an adult male (9)

21 Feeling poorly (6)

22 Harm, hurt (6)

DOWN

1 Sharp, bitter (taste) (6)

2 Statement requiring an answer (8)

3 In addition, besides (8)

4 Sucking parasites sometimes in human hair (4)

5 Pay for the use of something (4)

6 Prickly, spiny (6)

9 Suddenly disappearing from view (9)

13 Degree of slope on a road (8)

14 Kept secret (6,2)

15 Long piece of cloth wound round the head (6)

17 Done and ___, completely finished (6)

19 Date-bearing tree (4)

20 Unruly young girl (4)

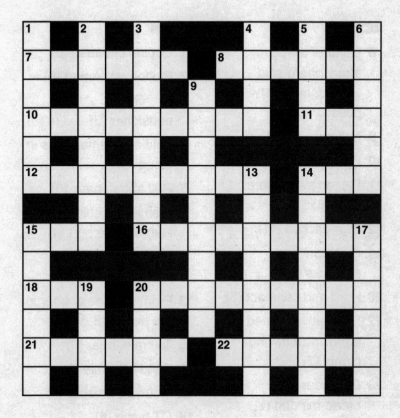

ACROSS

8 Layer of the atmosphere said to be damaged by pollution (5)

9 Normally (2,1,4)

10 Pulling suddenly (7)

11 Frozen sweet on a stick (5)

12 Jam-packed (11)

14 Problems and setbacks (11)

20 Hard and compact (5)

22 Decorative framed archway of trailing plants (7)

23 Generous or broad-minded (7)

24 Very necessary (5)

DOWN

1 Capital of Japan (5)

2 Plotted, schemed (8)

3 ___ citizen, old-age pensioner (6)

4 Wild animal that lives in a sett (6)

5 Roll about, bask (6)

6 Frame of a ship or a Humberside port (4)

7 Blue-green gem, or woman's name (5)

13 Premolar's neighbour in the mouth (3-5)

15 Tolerate, bear (6)

16 Bendy, flexible (6)

17 Flourish, prosper (6)

18 OT hymn (5)

19 First name of Hollywood star Ms Berry (5)

21 Ear part (4)

Sun

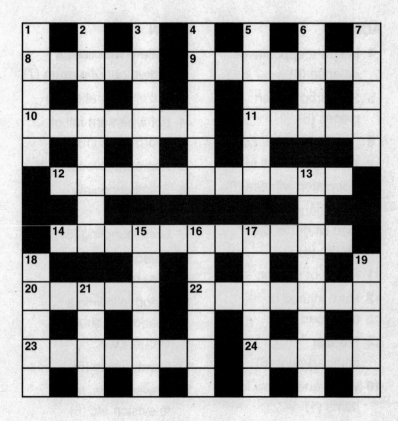

ACROSS

1 In sport, opposite of defence (6)

5 Scattered broken pieces (6)

8 ___ Thompson, *Love Actually* actress (4)

9 Spectator, witness (8)

10 Rock band whose lead singer is Chris Martin (8)

11 Minim or quaver, eg (4)

12 Hurt, injured or damaged (6)

14 Freezer compartment (6)

16 White and yellow food items (4)

18 Approximate judgement of number (8)

20 30-day month (8)

21 Measure of whisky (4)

22 Thinly dispersed (6)

23 Protected from bright light (6)

DOWN

2 Lottery with tickets picked out of a drum (7)

3 Prize, decoration (5)

4 (Of a person) full of information (13)

5 Assorted sweets (5,8)

6 Small chocolate cake (7)

7 Unfit, bungling (5)

13 Person who kneads sore muscles (7)

15 Mood following a scandal or shocking event (7)

17 Band, crowd (5)

19 Newspapers, radio, television etc (5)

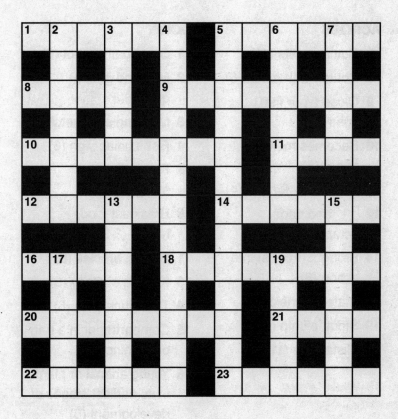

ACROSS

7 Cutting costs (11)

8 Coated with metal (6)

9 Close (your fist) tightly (6)

10 Becomes more sheer (8)

11 Metal tube for gas (4)

12 ___ and ends, scraps (4)

14 Brought (troops) into action (8)

17 State of tension (6)

19 Stout, plump (6)

20 Mistakenly (11)

DOWN

1 Small ball of shot (6)

2 Mild and gentle quality (8)

3 Meaningless sketch (6)

4 Fish zodiac sign (6)

5 Flying toy on a string (4)

6 Breakfast food holder (3-3)

11 Goods, articles (8)

13 Keep in custody (6)

14 Take guns from (6)

15 Compartment in a bag or clothing (6)

16 Young animal or plant in its earliest stages of development (6)

18 ___ and every, all (4)

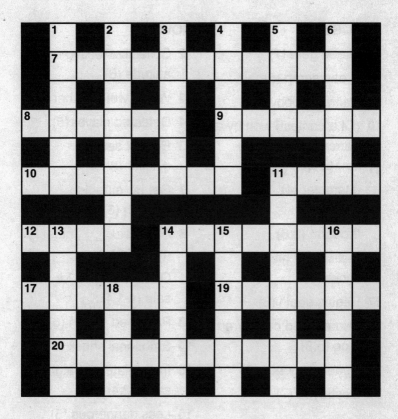

ACROSS

1 Green gem (7)

5 Bread scrap (5)

9 Railway hobby (13)

10 (Of a contest) won by a narrow margin (5-3)

11 ___ Bunny, cartoon character (4)

12 Perish the thought! (3,6)

16 Instrument hit with sticks (4)

17 Begins again (8)

19 Overcooked or charred food (5,8)

21 Speed, urgency (5)

22 Destroyed (7)

DOWN

2 Collective feeling or attitude (6)

3 Windy wet weather (9)

4 Defeated player (5)

6 Rodent sewer dweller (3)

7 Get by, muddle through (6)

8 *Little Jack* ___, nursery rhyme (6)

11 Odds and ends for sale (4-1-4)

13 Ploughed trench (6)

14 Emotional shock (6)

15 Immediately, straight away (2,4)

18 Less dangerous (5)

20 Word that makes a sentence negative (3)

ACROSS

1 Small spring flowers (8)

6 Opposite of 'thick' (4)

8 Run in tights (6)

9 Back of the neck, or untidy person (6)

10 Deprived of weapons (8)

13 Distort (4)

14 Entrance fee (9)

17 Entrance in a wall (4)

18 Whirling motion (8)

19 Soccer club's masseur (6)

21 Tainted, unclean (6)

23 Removed trapped air from (a radiator) (4)

24 Funds, sponsors (8)

DOWN

2 Part of the crew of a touring band (6)

3 Rotter, bounder (3)

4 Watching the pennies (9)

5 Distress call (inits)(3)

6 Evicted, expelled (6,3)

7 Notify, tell (6)

11 Wrote postal details on (an envelope) (9)

12 Act of going AWOL (9)

15 *My Cousin* ___, Daphne Du Maurier novel (6)

16 Unable to speak, as having a sore throat (6)

20 Clumsy fool (3)

22 Dressmaker's temporary fastener (3)

ACROSS

1 Round red-rinded Dutch cheese (4)

4 Ocean between Britain and America (8)

8 Wide tree-lined street (6)

9 Plant growing near mountain tops (6)

10 Slimy garden pest (4)

11 Holding up, making late (8)

13 Destroy (a town) (4,3,3,3)

16 Casing that a bird hatches from (8)

19 Crush food between the teeth (4)

20 Skimpy two-piece swimsuit (6)

22 Serviette (6)

23 Gas which combines with oxygen to make water (8)

24 Uses a spade (4)

DOWN

2 Reducing the worth of (9)

3 Surname of Australian singer Kylie (7)

4 At the front (5)

5 Thin brochure (7)

6 Chilly or quick (5)

7 Small hotel or pub (3)

12 Tidying (9)

14 Sensation (7)

15 Got away, broke free (7)

17 Winter sportsman (5)

18 Easily creased cloth (5)

21 Covered with frozen water (3)

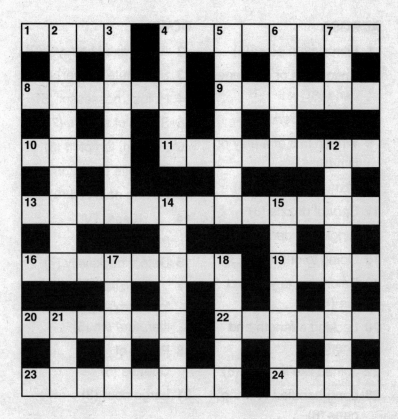

THE **Sun**

ACROSS

1 Film's main actor (4)

4 Antiquated or no longer used (8)

8 Teaching period (6)

9 Written text of a play or film (6)

10 Mark of a wound (4)

11 Spot of drizzle (8)

13 Single-mindedness (13)

16 Going to ground (5,3)

19 Belonging to you and me (4)

20 Lacking strength and energy (6)

22 Joined like a chain (6)

23 Long-handled stewing pans (8)

24 Simple (4)

DOWN

2 Act of wilful betrayal (9)

3 Substitute (player) (7)

4 Holder, possessor (5)

5 Series of sittings (7)

6 Enticed, tempted (5)

7 Opposite of 'bottom' (3)

12 Having no smell (9)

14 ___ Klass, TV presenter (7)

15 Defeat decisively (7)

17 ___ Prizes, awards for chemistry, peace, literature etc (5)

18 Prince of ___, Charles (5)

21 Large deer (3)

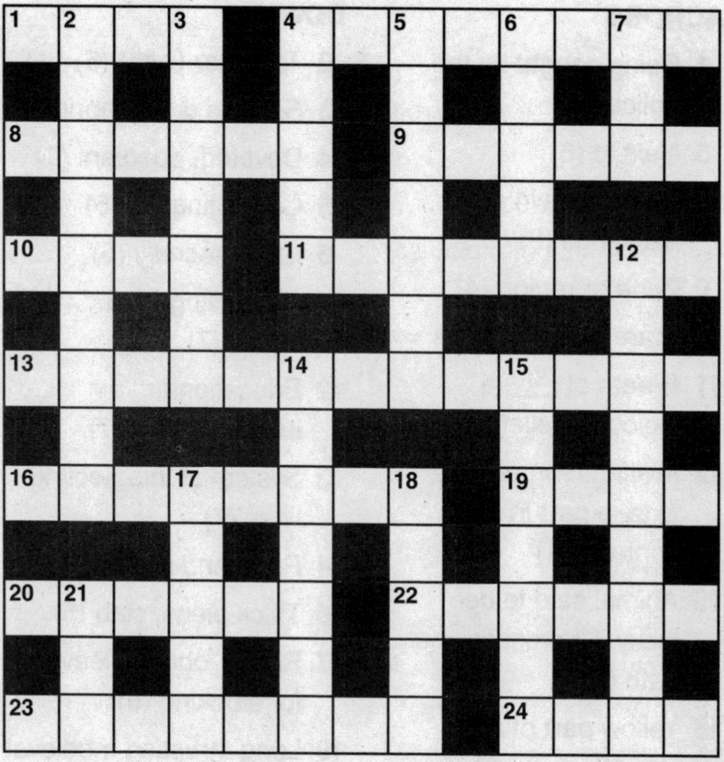

ACROSS

1 Being sought by the police (6)

5 Next to (6)

8 Paper thrown at weddings (8)

9 Zone or region (4)

10 Stare at lustfully (4)

11 Breath of ___, a welcome relief (5,3)

12 Inviting (someone) to take part in a contest (11)

15 Animal said to be lucky if it crosses your path (5,3)

18 Yellow part of an egg (4)

20 Choice of dishes in a restaurant (4)

21 Making an angry noise in the throat (8)

22 Drinking cup or mug (6)

23 Hit with the foot (6)

DOWN

2 Together (with) (5)

3 Silk-like dress fabric (7)

4 Devoted, obedient (7)

5 Corrupting gift (5)

6 Store secretly (5)

7 Controlling food intake (7)

12 Educational establishment (7)

13 System of intersecting lines (7)

14 Rural and unspoilt (7)

16 Thick piece, slab (5)

17 Roll of tobacco leaves for smoking (5)

19 Long thrusting medieval weapon (5)

ACROSS

7 Gymnast's close-fitting costume (7)

9 Common, typical (5)

10 ___ up, command to a horse (3)

11 Planned a route (9)

12 Brightly coloured spring flower (5)

14 On neither side, impartial (7)

16 Plant with pink stalks (7)

18 ___ energy, power from the Sun (5)

19 Pierce through (9)

20 Glossy fabric, used for macs (inits)(3)

21 1990s group fronted by brothers Liam and Noel Gallagher (5)

22 Crafty, sly (7)

DOWN

1 Friendly term for a pest (8)

2 Second to ___, the best (4)

3 Short sleep (6)

4 Martial art developed in China (4,2)

5 Relating to the arts (8)

6 Walk slowly and heavily (4)

8 Flexible plank at the edge of a swimming pool (6,5)

13 Amount of decibels (8)

15 Songwriter (8)

17 Picasso or Van Gogh, for example (6)

18 Change direction suddenly (6)

19 Having little or no money (4)

20 Item of stage equipment (4)

ACROSS

7 Rear entrance to a house (4,4)

8 Slightly chilly (4)

9 Hot pepper (6)

10 Occasions (5)

11 Correct, check (a text) (4)

12 Cars' waste-disposal systems (8)

14 Extending across (a river, eg) (8)

18 ___ of the valley, white flower (4)

20 Watchful, wide awake (5)

22 Leave (premises) (6)

23 Organ for breathing (4)

24 Rolled into a ball (6,2)

DOWN

1 Creamed (potatoes) (6)

2 Human framework (8)

3 Reason (for a crime) (6)

4 Miserable or pitiful person (6)

5 Dirty froth or foam (4)

6 Stiff undergarment (6)

13 Opened with a key (8)

15 ___ butter, popular spread (6)

16 Unbroken, complete (6)

17 Run (a country) (6)

19 Release (a prisoner) from jail (3,3)

21 Highly strung, twitchy (4)

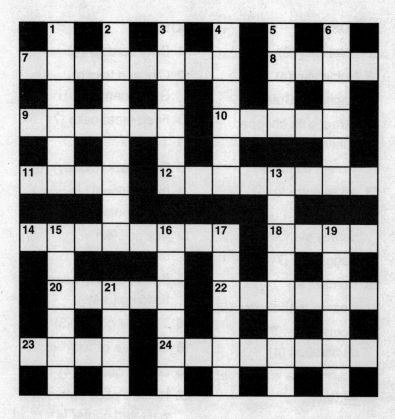

ACROSS

7 Total idiot (8)

8 Noble title (4)

9 Capital of Greece (6)

10 Sweet with chopped nuts (6)

11 Violent attack (7)

13 Allow entry to (5)

15 ___ Cross, London railway station (5)

17 Sogginess (7)

19 Hamper (6)

21 Heat or friendliness (6)

23 Courtroom declaration (4)

24 Start where another left off (6,2)

DOWN

1 Dirty humour (4)

2 City and lake of Switzerland (6)

3 Fried meat-cake (7)

4 Tilt (4)

5 Give back (money) (6)

6 International agreements (8)

12 In a coil-like movement (8)

14 Barrier to stop coastal flooding (3,4)

16 TV style guru (3,3)

18 Opposite of 'wide' (6)

20 Lovers' quarrel (4)

22 Horse's pace between walk and canter (4)

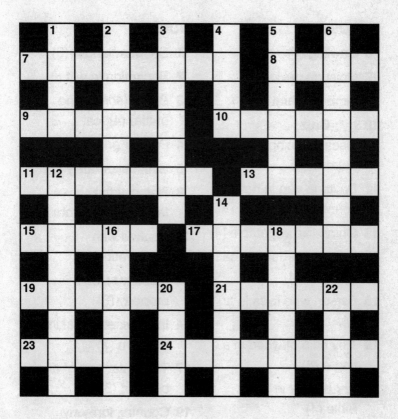

ACROSS

6 Bawling (7)

7 Hoisting device (5)

9 Limb of a bird (4)

10 ___ Cruz, Oscar-winning actress (8)

11 Daytime nap in hot countries (6)

13 Onion-like vegetable (4)

15 Instrument used to call to meals (4)

16 Person who lives in an igloo (6)

18 Tiny chip of wood in a finger (8)

21 Ark-builder in the Bible (4)

22 Whole amount (5)

23 Sign erected outside a house by an estate agent (3,4)

DOWN

1 Serious danger (5)

2 Beginning to wilt (8)

3 Break (something brittle) (4)

4 Pepper grinder (4)

5 Sink deliberately (7)

8 Remove the face-covering from (6)

12 Soaked with perspiration (6)

13 Inability to walk properly (8)

14 Improvised speaking platform (7)

17 Triangular end of a building (5)

19 Country, formerly Persia (4)

20 Top of a building (4)

ACROSS

1 Hoards, gathers (supplies) (10)
8 Of water, salty (5)
9 British language (7)
10 Series of boat races (7)
11 Give an answer in speech or writing (5)
12 Someone who digs the dirt (4-5)
15 Take exams again (5)
17 Wear away by chemical action (7)
19 Bedding item (7)
20 Full of flavour (5)
21 Leaving for good (10)

DOWN

2 Item (5)
3 Variety of crossword clue (7)
4 Manufactured in pieces for assembly on site (13)
5 Light beer of German origin (5)
6 Comfy indoor shoe (7)
7 Those people (4)
8 In the buff (4)
12 Eye make-up (7)
13 First name of actress Ms Dunst (7)
14 Refuse to admit (4)
15 Red stone (4)
16 Chicken ___ masala, popular Indian dish (5)
18 ___ Welles, American film actor and director (5)

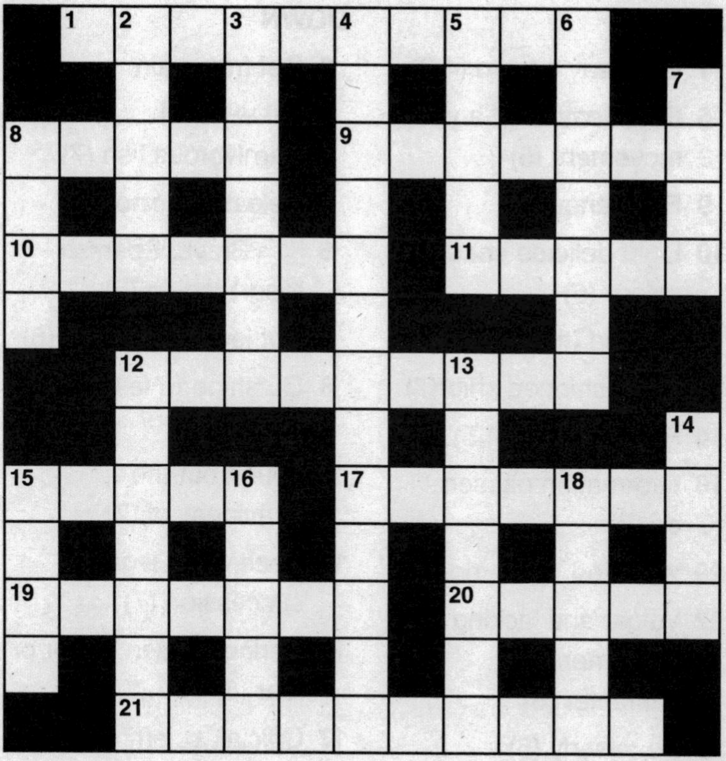
1
2
3
4
5
6
7
8
9
10
11
12
13
14
15
16
17
18
19
20
21

ACROSS

1 Don't say a word (4,3)

5 Boy member of a youth movement (5)

9 Frightened (6)

10 Light delicate shade of colour (6)

11 Passed (time) (5)

12 Old-fashioned ship (7)

14 Repeat order (4,5)

18 Information passed on (7)

20 Wobbled, quivered (5)

22 Vulgar and lacking refinement of character (6)

23 Be miserly (6)

24 Water chute at a theme park (5)

25 Fragile, easily snapped (7)

DOWN

2 Get free, gain freedom (6)

3 Carnivorous fish (7)

4 Release (a knot) (4)

6 ___ Brava, Spanish resort region (5)

7 Not level or smooth (6)

8 Outshine (a fellow actor) (7)

13 Found out the heaviness of (7)

15 Receive by legal succession (7)

16 Spring back in horror or fear (6)

17 Official, solemn (6)

19 Clear off! (5)

21 One who consumes or operates (4)

ACROSS

1 Used a pen (5)

4 Corn or wheat, for example (5)

9 Confine in a camp during wartime (6)

10 Musical note (6)

12 Power tool for boring holes (8,5)

13 Lasting for too much time (7)

18 Method of setting hair in curls that will not drop out (9,4)

19 Walk like a small child (6)

20 Young porker (6)

21 Conflict (5)

22 Pore over books (5)

DOWN

2 Fairly, somewhat (6)

3 Completely reverse a situation (4,3,6)

5 Crazy, mad (5,3,5)

6 Pointlessly, fruitlessly (2,4)

7 Large watercourse (5)

8 Cook or interrogate (5)

11 Sleeveless vest (7)

14 Desire to hurt or annoy someone (5)

15 ___ suite, honeymooners' hotel rooms (6)

16 Travelled by boat (6)

17 Small-minded, trivial (5)

ACROSS

3 Drop in the middle (3)

7 Having no unoccupied space (4,2)

8 Dried grape (6)

9 Proposal to be voted on in a debate (6)

10 Fisherman (6)

11 Machine for making books, newspapers etc (8,5)

13 Same size as in reality (2,5,2,4)

18 Threadbare, worn out (6)

19 Very dry region (6)

20 Scary type of film (6)

21 Of a traffic system, moving in a single direction (3-3)

22 Granny (3)

DOWN

1 Piece of unverified gossip (6)

2 West Bromwich ___, football team (6)

3 Relating a shaggy-dog story (8,1,4)

4 Male relative three generations younger (5-8)

5 Hang about (6)

6 Muscle at the front of the upper arm (6)

11 Tiny vegetable (3)

12 View, look at (3)

14 Place of learning (6)

15 Husband of Queen Victoria (6)

16 Pay attention (6)

17 Layout, structure (6)

21 Bromide's crop (6)
22 ___ unprocessing (6)
23 Become more
dense, thick (6)

14 Hangs a nose ahead,
asleep due to breaking
through the image (13)
19 Forest within (8)

THE Sun

ACROSS

5 Causing a lasting emotional shock (9)

8 Disappear from sight (6)

9 James ___, film star noted for his gangster roles (6)

10 Form of the verb 'to be' (3)

11 Twitch and twiddle restlessly (6)

13 Most uncommon (6)

15 Gary ___, Take That singer (6)

18 Deep sadness (6)

20 Hurried along (3)

21 Move in a circle (6)

22 ___ up, confessing (6)

23 Became more dense (9)

DOWN

1 Using a towel (6)

2 Head protection in hot weather (3,3)

3 Zodiac sign of the Crab (6)

4 Hand digit (6)

6 Co-driver in a car rally (9)

7 Small stirring utensils (9)

12 Self-importance (3)

14 In days gone by (3)

16 Regard with hatred and disgust (6)

17 Sudden violent twist or pull (6)

18 Made a noise when asleep due to breathing through the mouth (6)

19 Forest warden (6)

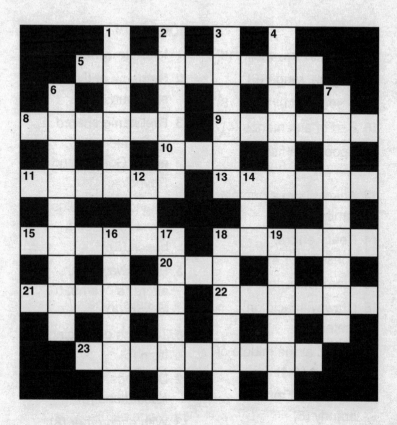

ACROSS

7 Enthusiasm, vitality (6)

8 Degree, range (6)

9 Wooden sculptures (8)

10 Part of a sentence (4)

11 Spool for a fishing line (4)

12 Animal from a primate family (5,3)

14 Really enjoyed oneself (3,1,4)

16 Stern, cheerless (4)

18 Draw with acid on metal (4)

20 Period at the middle of a game (4-4)

22 Variety of French brandy (6)

23 Paint colour that can be raw or burnt (6)

DOWN

1 Infuriate, madden (6)

2 Surname of *Grease* star John (8)

3 First name shared by Canadian actors Gosling and Reynolds (4)

4 Abandoned mollusc cover found on a beach (8)

5 Pack away (in an aircraft's overhead locker) (4)

6 Take the packaging from (6)

12 Drawings, illustrations (8)

13 With each other (8)

15 Novel's creator (6)

17 Having natural protection from a disease (6)

19 Good-looking man (4)

21 Strike with a whip (4)

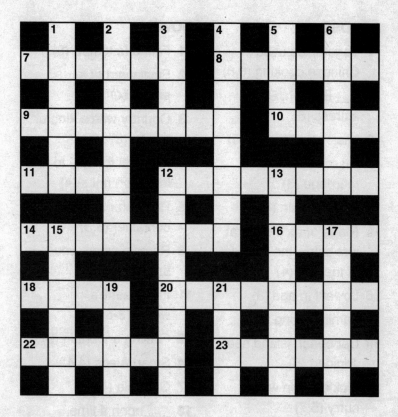

ACROSS

7 Vegetables used in Chinese cooking (6,6)

8 ___ Blethyn, British actress (6)

9 Miss ___, Muppet (5)

10 Dissolved a marriage (8)

13 Round basin (4)

15 Ridge of rock or coral just below the surface of the sea (4)

16 Lowest in age (8)

17 Family saying (5)

19 Caribbean island near Trinidad (6)

21 Pickle eaten with curry (5,7)

DOWN

1 Failed (attempt) (8)

2 Final word of a prayer (4)

3 Country with a king or queen (8)

4 Request to reply to an invitation (inits)(4)

5 Restaurant leftovers container (5,3)

6 Remain where you are (4)

11 In a theatre's wings (3-5)

12 Feeling uncertain (8)

14 Smart Alecs (4,4)

17 Grumble (4)

18 ___ upon a time, fairy-tale opening (4)

20 Any part of a skeleton (4)

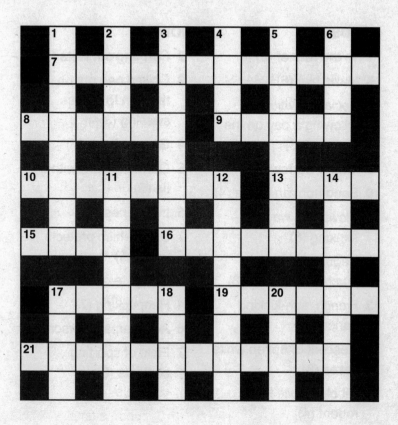

ACROSS

1 To the rear of (6)

5 Mark, blot (6)

8 Social activities following a day on the slopes (5-3)

9 Money borrowed (4)

10 Song from an opera (4)

11 Viewpoint, way of thinking (8)

12 Regular cigarette purchaser or user (6)

13 French high-kicking dance (6)

15 Descent of frozen white flakes (8)

18 Nibble or bite like a rodent (4)

19 Movie (4)

20 Dangly jewellery items (8)

21 Meeting's programme (6)

22 Duffel-coat fastening (6)

DOWN

2 Carrying out tests (13)

3 Chilled bag put on the skin to reduce swelling (3,4)

4 Give up hope (7)

5 Garment worn with a tie (5)

6 In darkness (5)

7 Spirit which protects you (8,5)

13 Guilty person (7)

14 Henpecking (7)

16 Adult female person (5)

17 Field of sporting contests (5)

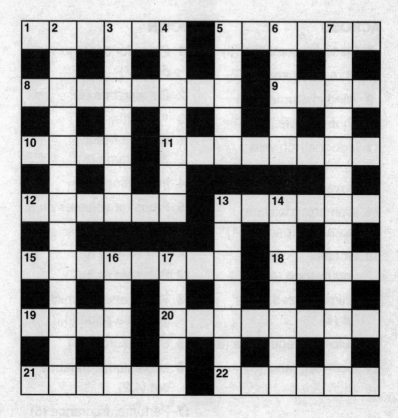

ACROSS

7 Place for gambling (6)

8 Burn while ironing (6)

9 Wind instrument (4)

10 Footsloggers (8)

11 Indoor shrub with dark-green shiny leaves (6,5)

14 Woman's matching jacket and pants (7,4)

18 Got off ___, went unpunished (4-4)

19 Animal prized for its fur (4)

20 Bulb-like vegetables (6)

21 Incorrect, false (6)

DOWN

1 Place for boats to dock (7)

2 Go upwards (4)

3 ___ Who, science-fiction programme (6)

4 In addition (2,4)

5 Props for volumes on a shelf (4-4)

6 Hair-raising (5)

12 Pub seat (3,5)

13 Young animal which lives in a pride (4,3)

15 Civil disorder (6)

16 Make equal, balance out (4,2)

17 Perfume, fragrance (5)

19 Insect attracted to light (4)

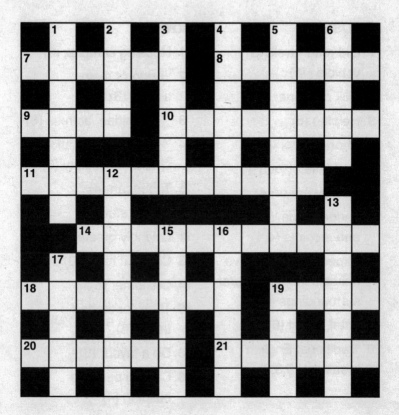

ACROSS

7 Old road-levelling vehicle (11)

8 Milk container (6)

9 Helping (6)

10 Shortest month (8)

11 Opposite of 'odd' (4)

12 Was aware of (4)

14 Ledger of payments and receipts (4,4)

17 Expedition to observe animals in their natural surroundings (6)

19 Fatal, lethal (6)

20 Traditional English breakfast (5,3,3)

DOWN

1 Housing complex (6)

2 London's main airport (8)

3 ___ Holden, actress (6)

4 ___ Club, international charitable society (6)

5 Toboggan (4)

6 Dazed state (6)

11 Lovingly greeted (8)

13 Close at hand (6)

14 Customer (6)

15 Track for storing trains (6)

16 Do a favour (6)

18 Curved part of a building (4)

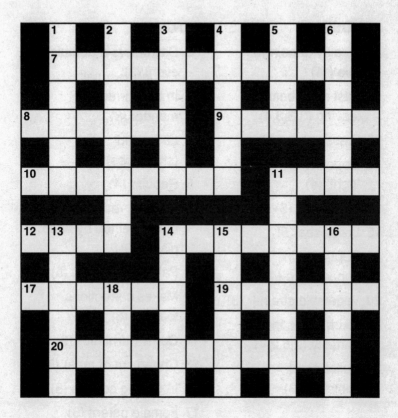

ACROSS

1 Quality of being of use (11)

9 Last drink before leaving (3,3,3,4)

10 Presses hard (8)

12 Opposite of 'right' (4)

14 Make cold (5)

15 Large sea (5)

19 Repulsive in appearance (4)

20 Vegetable strainer (8)

22 To be frank, in all honesty (2,5,2,4)

24 Bullet-proof vehicle (8,3)

DOWN

2 Day before a notable event (3)

3 In the correct manner (8)

4 Loosened (shoelaces) (6)

5 Require (4)

6 In sport, record of points gained by each player (9)

7 Pale-brown (hair) (5)

8 Makes corrections to (text) (5)

11 Cover (furniture) (9)

13 Cheap cut of meat (5-3)

16 In glaring colours (5)

17 Female parent (6)

18 Name for a group of lions (5)

21 Board-game with counters (4)

23 Egg cells (3)

ACROSS

1 Icy coating on the top layer of soil (6,5)

9 Pole used to row a boat (3)

10 Fine white porcelain (4,5)

11 Frail, sickly (8)

12 Departs this life (4)

14 Leather seat for a horse rider (6)

16 Eastern robe (6)

18 Underground part of a plant (4)

19 Not tried and tested (8)

22 In childbirth, born before time (9)

23 Fuel used for cooking and heating (3)

24 Tutor's favourite (8,3)

DOWN

2 To do with the countryside (5)

3 Loosen (a belt) (8)

4 Give (blood) (6)

5 Possessing great wealth (4)

6 Easy route to a mountain summit (3-4)

7 Dull, featureless (11)

8 Fatty extremity of a cooked chicken's rump (7,4)

13 Justice, impartiality (8)

15 Bishop's area (7)

17 Not certain (6)

20 Style, fashion (5)

21 Bathroom powder (4)

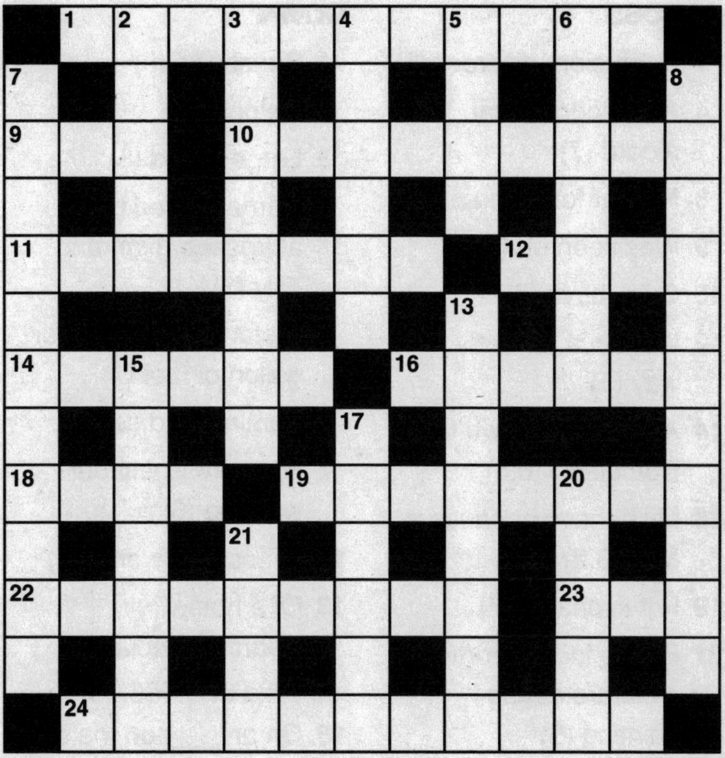

ACROSS

1 Confusion, disorder (5)
4 Autobiographical record (7)
8 Feeder for a horse (7)
9 Was keen on (5)
10 Own, have (7)
12 Walk in a leisurely way (5)
14 Actor best known for *Homeland* (6,5)
18 Misbehave or cause a fuss (3,2)
19 Put in chains (7)
21 Frame for supporting a picture during painting (5)
23 Surname of Hollywood star Julia (7)
24 Go off at a ___, digress (7)
25 ___ wave, great surge of water (5)

DOWN

1 Sunshade (6)
2 Helper (9)
3 Large sword (5)
4 Name shared by actresses Ryan and Tilly (3)
5 Distance travelled per gallon of fuel (7)
6 Printing fluid (3)
7 Happening without warning (6)
11 Tunes with words (5)
13 Of a horse, wearing special eye-coverings (9)
15 On an ___, on the spur of the moment (7)
16 Mother or father (6)
17 *Pop Goes the* ___, nursery rhyme (6)
20 Monastery head (5)
22 Biblical wrong (3)
23 Decay (3)

ACROSS

1 Unwilling to share (7)
5 Antlered deer (4)
10 Top Twenty record (3)
11 Copy, duplicate (9)
12 Burn slightly (5)
13 Regular religious ceremony (6)
15 Day nursery (6)
17 ___ Puddleduck, Beatrix Potter character (6)
18 Continue, maintain (4,2)
20 Sludge (5)
23 Lack of guilt (9)
24 Promise of payment (inits)(3)
25 Lazy (4)
26 Nation, land (7)

DOWN

2 ___ John, knighted pop pianist (5)
3 Make everyone go faster (5,3,4)
4 Really good (5)
6 Tidal wave caused by an earthquake (7)
7 Stacey's mum in *Gavin & Stacey* (4)
8 School science subject (7)
9 Opposite point to 'north-western' (5-7)
14 Unable or not needing to sleep (7)
16 Never-ending (7)
19 *Aladdin* or *Puss in Boots*, eg (5)
21 Chillier (5)
22 Stereo equipment (2-2)

ACROSS

1 Ingredients and cooking method for a dish (6)
4 Olympic throwing event (6)
9 UK TV company (inits) (3)
10 No matter what (2,3,4)
11 Happy or friendly facial expression (5)
12 Turned sour (of milk) (7)
14 Farming of the land (11)
17 Untidy bits and bobs (7)
18 Different, alternative (5)
20 People in custody (9)
22 Chris ___, *The Road to Hell* singer (3)
23 Large fuel-carrying ship (6)
24 Nervous and jittery (2,4)

DOWN

1 Strong, sturdy (6)
2 Spiny plants found in the desert (5)
3 Catalogue of charges (5,4)
5 Wall-climbing plant (3)
6 Toady, yes-man (7)
7 Use cash (5)
8 Safe havens (11)
13 Chemical substance used to kill rodents (3,6)
15 Person who eats excessively (7)
16 Invent, make (6)
17 Trainee soldier (5)
19 Rented (a car, eg) (5)
21 Drink cooler (3)

ACROSS

8 Engage as a participant (7)

9 ___ Marbles, Parthenon sculptures (5)

10 Kitchen garment (5)

11 Below freezing (3-4)

12 Tempt fate (4,4,4)

16 White substance applied after a bath (6,6)

20 Cover by wrapping (7)

23 Truck (5)

24 Punctuation mark separating a list of items (5)

25 Substance in food that aids growth (7)

DOWN

1 Church of England minister (5)

2 Stuffed to excess (8)

3 Draw back in fear (6)

4 Items for hanging up washing (4)

5 Person belonging to a particular society or group (6)

6 Fairy-tale giant (4)

7 Opens (a wine bottle) (7)

13 Retired person (inits)(3)

14 ___ income, money from a source other than work (8)

15 Extend, like elastic (7)

17 Empty (a truck) (6)

18 Weeping ___, drooping tree (6)

19 Animal well known for its laugh-like sound (5)

21 Alluring seductress (4)

22 Fruit seeds (4)

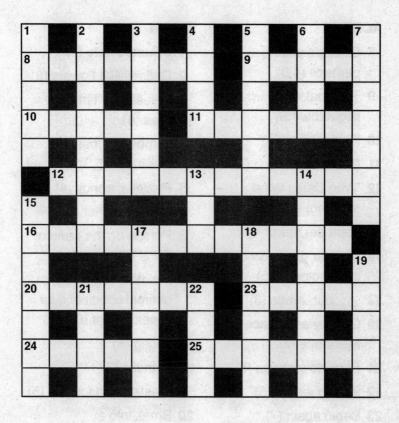

ACROSS

7 Grizzly's young, perhaps (4,3)

9 Tear-making vegetable (5)

10 Ride a bike (5)

11 Devour too much (7)

12 'Who Dares Wins' regiment (inits)(3)

13 Improper, lewd (8)

16 Circular graph divided into sectors (3,5)

17 ___ out, erase (3)

19 Occupy as a place of residence (7)

21 Seaside features (5)

22 Sailing vessel (5)

23 Begin again (7)

DOWN

1 Inflamed sore (7)

2 Daffodil-like flowers (8)

3 Measure of land area (4)

4 Temporary loss of electricity (5,3)

5 Provoke, annoy (4)

6 Bring together (5)

8 Person on the radio or TV (11)

13 Maintain (eggs, eg) at optimal conditions for development (8)

14 Viking (8)

15 Fatness (7)

18 Plastic used for LPs (5)

20 Break into a computer (4)

21 Small bunch of flowers (4)

ACROSS

7 Rained heavily (6)

8 Misused (6)

10 Alexander Graham Bell's invention (9)

11 Public vehicle (3)

12 State of poverty (9)

14 ___ up, admit (3)

15 Furrow made by wheels (3)

16 Table napkin (9)

18 Small number of (3)

20 Stop working in protest (4,5)

21 Name that links actors Butler and Depardieu (6)

22 Spoil the appearance of (6)

DOWN

1 Exactly right (4,2)

2 Most twisted (8)

3 Gives up hope (8)

4 Handed over (4)

5 Injure with a knife (4)

6 Better than even chance in betting (4-2)

9 From your garden (4-5)

13 Game played in an alley (8)

14 Voluntary, non-compulsory (8)

15 Place of safety (6)

17 Less complicated (6)

19 Hospital bedroom (4)

20 Mend (a woollen garment) (4)

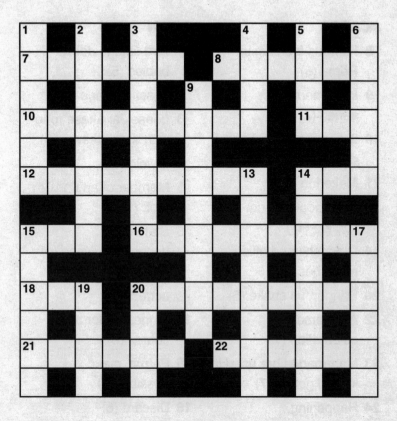

ACROSS

8 Famous fountain in Rome (5)

9 Instalment of a series (7)

10 Italian meat-filled pasta dish (7)

11 Make fun of (5)

12 (Of a booking) not verified (11)

14 Old-fashioned office machines (11)

20 Dangerous snake (5)

22 Anniversary celebration (7)

23 Man-made fibre used in knitted goods (7)

24 Happening, occurrence (5)

DOWN

1 Bird said to deliver babies (5)

2 Blissful, divine (8)

3 Loose Japanese robe with wide sleeves (6)

4 Opinion (6)

5 Member of an unruly mob (6)

6 State of unconsciousness (4)

7 ___ Zellweger, actress (5)

13 Signed up for a course (8)

15 Permit, make possible (6)

16 Discard (6)

17 Medicine in pill form (6)

18 Metal ready for recycling (5)

19 Triangular tract of land at a river's mouth (5)

21 Unruly son of TV's Homer and Marge Simpson (4)

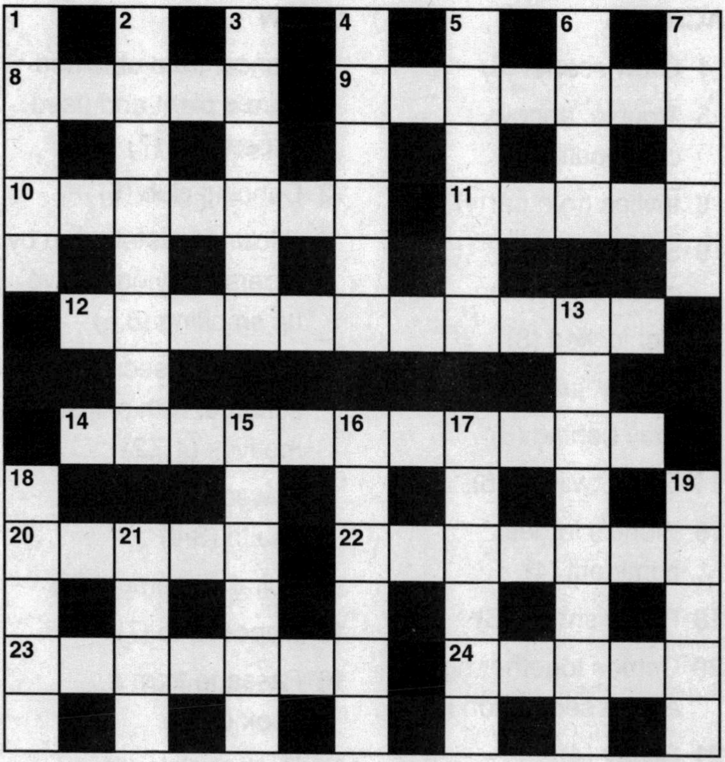

ACROSS

1 Grow scarlet (6)
5 Trouble, annoy continually (6)
8 Invites (to a party) (4)
9 Subsiding, collapsing (6,2)
10 Not locked (8)
11 Merely, just (4)
12 Stay behind (6)
14 Dusk, twilight (6)
16 World's largest continent (4)
18 Public shows (8)
20 Comes together again after a separation (8)
21 Stingy (4)
22 Rough drawing (6)
23 Nakedness, state of undress (6)

DOWN

2 Concentrate obtained from a plant and used in perfume (7)
3 Dancing club (5)
4 Sticking plaster worn by a person trying to give up smoking (8,5)
5 Contrive a secret scheme, with selfish motives (4,7,2)
6 In weakened health (3-4)
7 Spiral movement (5)
13 Opposed to (7)
15 Passage from a book (7)
17 Dust particle (5)
19 Intended, targeted (5)

ACROSS

1 Many a time (5)

4 Embarrassed (7)

9 Mexican hat (8)

10 Fine soft fabric (4)

11 Hey ___, magician's call (6)

12 Bind (a person) securely (3,2)

13 Similar to candle material (4)

15 Common dog command (3)

16 Animal that is hunted by another for food (4)

17 Black lumps for burning (5)

19 Hard work (6)

21 Look after or care about (4)

22 Unfit to eat (8)

23 Be subjected to, suffer (7)

24 Call the ___, make the decisions (5)

DOWN

2 Bread's main ingredient (5)

3 Ambassador's residence (7)

5 Charming flatterer (6-6)

6 Gap between rows of seats (5)

7 Shape like a flattened circle (7)

8 Taking back ownership (of a house, eg) (12)

14 Sale where bids are made (7)

16 Bring out in print (7)

18 ___ Agassi, former tennis star (5)

20 Vacant (property), without tenants (5)

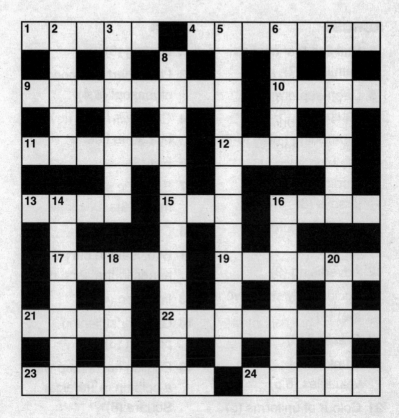

ACROSS

1 Building that houses paintings (7)

5 Deep-sea diving equipment (5)

9 Rib-tickling (joke) (5-8)

10 Clothing such as cardigans and jerseys (8)

11 Beasts of burden, cattle (4)

12 Advertising (9)

16 Accidentally strike (your toe) (4)

17 Crashed (8)

19 Trunk full of valuables (8,5)

21 Colour of uniforms (5)

22 Pursuing (7)

DOWN

2 Hurting (6)

3 Lamp part that needs changing! (5,4)

4 *Cider with* ___, novel by Laurie Lee (5)

6 Hat (3)

7 Sausage served with mash (6)

8 Cloth, textile (6)

11 Birds said to bury their heads in the sand (9)

13 Imprison (4,2)

14 Laundry stiffening product (6)

15 English naval hero with a column in Trafalgar Square (6)

18 Bloodsucking worm once used in medicine (5)

20 Boat which saved the animals (3)

ACROSS

1 In a frank way (8)

6 Wooden barrel used for liquor (4)

8 Event that will never happen again (3-3)

9 Protruded the lips sulkily (6)

10 Flower wreaths (8)

13 Money paid to the courts as security (4)

14 Directs (a boat) (9)

17 ___ Jackman, Australian actor (4)

18 Bestowing (8)

19 Soak up like a sponge (6)

21 Ran away to marry (6)

23 Extravagant publicity (4)

24 Grappling (8)

DOWN

2 Yearly comic book (6)

3 Stage twosome (3)

4 Protecting (9)

5 Small dog's bark (3)

6 Most plump (9)

7 Beautiful to look at (view) (6)

11 Hateful (9)

12 Ocean travellers (9)

15 Foaming, fizzy (6)

16 Invisible (6)

20 Games racket (3)

22 Substance obtained from olives (3)

ACROSS

1 Fifty per cent (4)

4 Happened again (8)

8 Crackling sound on a radio (6)

9 Have a meal away from home (3,3)

10 Medicinal substance or narcotic (4)

11 Gift given to children attending a birthday celebration (5,3)

13 Displeasing, distasteful (13)

16 Saviours (8)

19 Solemn undertaking to tell the truth (4)

20 Assert positively (6)

22 Bobbed the head in agreement (6)

23 Eccentric or strange people (8)

24 Statistics (4)

DOWN

2 Possible to change (9)

3 Tiredness (7)

4 Go over (the facts) again (5)

5 Goodbye! (7)

6 Have another bash (5)

7 Flightless bird (3)

12 Piece of land let by the council to grow your own vegetables (9)

14 Variety of underwear that keeps you extra-warm (7)

15 Steered clear of (7)

17 Scale (a ladder) (5)

18 Cavity connected to the nose (5)

21 Gave a meal to (3)

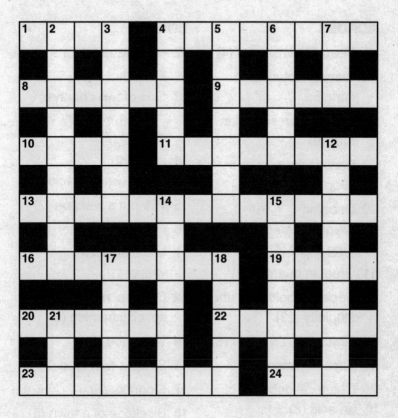

ACROSS

1 Beautiful white bird (4)

4 Wary of potential dangers (8)

8 Creature preserved in rock (6)

9 Canvas cover over a shop's front (6)

10 Deborah ___, Yul Brynner's co-star in *The King and I* (4)

11 Great in quantity (8)

13 Reckless boldness and stupidity (13)

16 Financially swindles (8)

19 Kitchen fitment (4)

20 Chemical opposite of an acid (6)

22 OK to eat (6)

23 Headlong rush (8)

24 Stay out of view (4)

DOWN

2 Healthy, good for you (9)

3 One of two channels through which air is inhaled (7)

4 ___ Firth, Oscar-winning actor (5)

5 Without a weapon (7)

6 Opposite of 'outer' (5)

7 Metal tea-making vessel (3)

12 Of a job, not calling for specific training (9)

14 Very rude (7)

15 Sustain with food (7)

17 Kingdom (5)

18 Blockade of a town (5)

21 Great amount (3)

ACROSS

1 Plane without an engine (6)

5 Means of acknowledging a superior officer (6)

8 Clean, germ-free (8)

9 Belonging to me (4)

10 Artificially coloured (4)

11 Become less amusing over time (4,4)

12 Form to send to a company for further details (5,6)

15 Makes firm, supports (8)

18 As well (4)

20 Senseless, foolish (4)

21 Bringing into existence (8)

22 Tight-fisted (6)

23 Go beyond (6)

DOWN

2 Roadside parking place (3-2)

3 Withered, shrivelled (5-2)

4 Fugitive, deserter (7)

5 ___ Baron Cohen, actor and comedian (5)

6 Restrict (5)

7 Nervous strain (7)

12 Withdraw, take back (7)

13 Coarse, lewd (7)

14 Light strong material often used for children's toys (7)

16 One more time (5)

17 In need of a scratch (5)

19 Somehow feel (5)

ACROSS

7 Pop star's followers (3,4)

9 Distribute in portions (5)

10 UK honour (inits)(3)

11 Chap who can tear telephone directories? (9)

12 Art of writing and presenting plays (5)

14 Issue of a publication (7)

16 'Best canine' competition (3,4)

18 Grain used to make bread (5)

19 In a fit condition to fly (9)

20 Gone bad (3)

21 Joint on which a door turns (5)

22 Regular daily habits (7)

DOWN

1 Had the financial means to buy (8)

2 Leg joint (4)

3 Type of TV, or part of the blood (6)

4 Kylie Minogue's younger sister (6)

5 ___ tonic, low-calorie drink (8)

6 Render senseless with a blow (4)

8 Fruit and grain soft drink (6,5)

13 Vexing, enraging (8)

15 Told, informed (8)

17 Curved down like an eagle's beak (6)

18 Exit (3,3)

19 Continuous dull pain (4)

20 Forget to include (4)

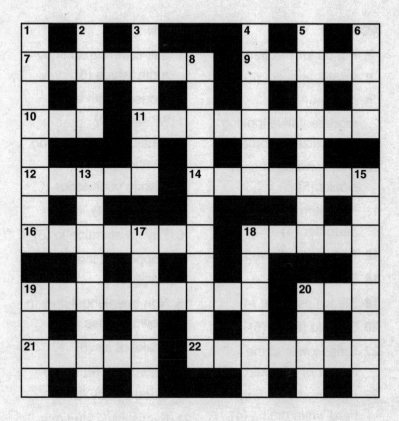

ACROSS

7 Put up for election (8)

8 Strong impulse (4)

9 Government representative looking after citizens abroad (6)

10 House made of snow blocks (5)

11 Elizabeth II's only daughter (4)

12 Accepted, allowed (8)

14 Possible (8)

18 Sleeveless coat (4)

20 Sample (food) (5)

22 Small tower at the corner of a building (6)

23 Pudding made from hard white grains (4)

24 Rushing streams of water (8)

DOWN

1 Silk covering spun by moth larvae (6)

2 Trousers with a low waistline (8)

3 Small, strong-smelling, onion-like bulb (6)

4 Give in your notice (6)

5 Haul, tug (4)

6 Pay no attention to (6)

13 Happened, took place (8)

15 Non-speaking actors in crowd scenes (6)

16 Intake of air (6)

17 Unbroken, whole (6)

19 Good supply (6)

21 Excessively studious pupil (4)

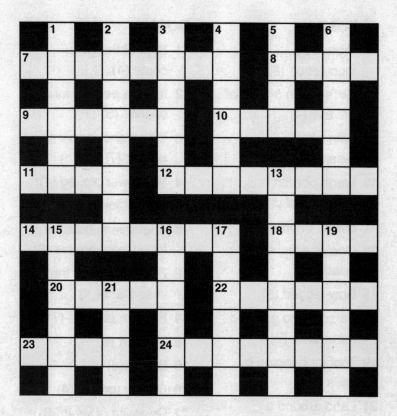

ACROSS

7 Protect by inoculation (8)

8 Girl's name or part of the eye (4)

9 With no resemblance (6)

10 Large portion or lump (eg of cream) (6)

11 Boffin, brainbox (7)

13 One of a flight of treads (5)

15 Bow-legged (5)

17 Person who goes up mountains (7)

19 Tool for banging in nails (6)

21 Land around a house (6)

23 Transferred unit of heredity (4)

24 Purple gemstone (8)

DOWN

1 Sign of things to come (4)

2 Inflict a penalty for an offence (6)

3 Emergency service worker (7)

4 Sunflower pip, eg (4)

5 Purple flower (6)

6 Addictive substance found in cigarettes (8)

12 Zone in front of the net in soccer (4,4)

14 Filled in (a hole) (7)

16 Moisten (6)

18 Boggy (6)

20 Gather (crops) (4)

22 Opposite of west (4)

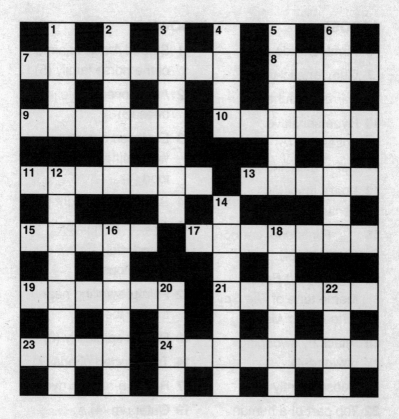

ACROSS

6 Firmly decide (7)

7 Gum for sticking (5)

9 Barren, parched (4)

10 Hypersensitive, obsessive (8)

11 Bet at a casino (6)

13 Poet's inspiring genius (4)

15 ___ Flintstone, cartoon character (4)

16 ___ *Does It Better*, theme tune of *The Spy Who Loved Me* (6)

18 Attack by swooping down (4-4)

21 Subsequently (4)

22 Top part of a human leg (5)

23 Floating through the air (7)

DOWN

1 Striped African animal of the horse family (5)

2 Area covered in trees (8)

3 Enclosed compartment for heating or cooking food (4)

4 Saint's ring of light (4)

5 To start with (2,5)

8 Wonderful, marvellous (6)

12 Painful swelling near the big toe (6)

13 Reflect spiritually (8)

14 Transported goods (7)

17 Reddish-orange dye (5)

19 Outer rim (4)

20 One-sidedness (4)

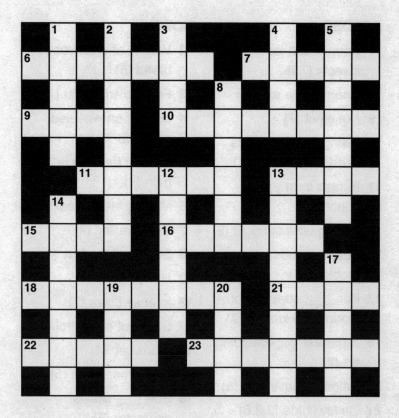

ACROSS

1 Spun snare for trapping insects (7,3)

8 Room in the roof (5)

9 Not strict (7)

10 Swing-like apparatus used by acrobats (7)

11 Banish from your country (5)

12 Putting up a struggle (9)

15 Puzzling question or problem (5)

17 Ben ___, co-writer of *Good Will Hunting* (7)

19 Japanese paper-folding art (7)

20 Reigned, governed (5)

21 Lie low, hide (2,2,6)

DOWN

2 Variety of unleavened bread (5)

3 Female aristocrat (7)

4 Moving on wheeled shoes (6-7)

5 Contort the face in pain (5)

6 Making tea or beer (7)

7 Eye swelling (4)

8 Sections of a play (4)

12 Hurrying (7)

13 Intense blaze (7)

14 Slide out of control (4)

15 Elbow jab (4)

16 Cook in an oven (5)

18 Sue ___, *Dallas* character (5)

No. 1

```
  A S A   T   D W
B O N F I R E N I G H T
R   A   R X   S   E
C A M P U S   T A C K Y
S       T     I
D I S C A R D S   P O O R
V   R   I   P   L   R
F E T A   P R E S E N C E
    N       E     H
  S W E D E   D E F E A T
O   F   C   W   A   R
W H O L E H E A R T E D
O   Y   O   Y   E   S
```

No. 2

```
A D V E N T   A C C U S E
O   A   W   N   O   T
S L U R P I N G   H O R N
L   S   T   L   E   A
M Y T H   C L E A N I N G
M   O   H           G
F I L T H Y   C A G N E Y
X           L   A   T
S T A M P E D E   S M O G
U   A   I   A   T   T
G R A N   G O V E R N E D
E   G   H   E   I   L
E S C O R T   R E C A L L
```

No. 3

```
  L   I G   J D   T
T O D D L E   A T O M I C
G   L   O   G   O   R
H I V E   R E G A R D E D
C   B   G   E   K   D
H A P P Y E N D I N G
  L   R       O   S
    D O U B L E D B A C K
N   T   U   X       R
H O R R I F I C   S E A N
V   U   F   E L   P
M E D D L E   E X I T E D
  L   E   T D D   R
```

No. 4

```
  S   I B H   D A
C O M M U N I T I E S
O   M   L   D M   T
S T R O L L   D I E O U T
C   B   E   E   T   T
C H R I S T E N   B L E W
      L       L
O B O E   C A P T I O N S
L   H   L   S   I
B O W T I E   A S S E N T
U   A   E   I   F   E
S Q U A S H C O U R T
E   T   E   E L   Y
```

No. 5

```
  T E M P E R A T U R E
C   E   R   A Y O   A
H A L L O F M I R R O R S
U   T   S E   M   H
C A B L E C A R   N I C E
K   A   I Y   C N   S
  A L O N E   L A T E X
G   L   S A R   S   A
U R G E   S T R E S S E D
E   I   T H   F   A
S T R A W B E R R Y J A M
T   L   E N   E U   S
  A S S E S S M E N T S
```

No. 6

```
  S C A R E D S T I F F
W   A E   R   I R   C
A T M   O V E R R E A C H
R   E   P A   E G   A
M U L B E R R Y   L I O N
E   N   Y I   L   G
M A S H E D   S N E E Z E
O   U   D C   P     H
R U B Y   C H A R I S M A
I   A   S A   I H   N
A C Q U A I N T S   O L D
L   U   L C   O C   S
  R A T T L E S N A K E
```

No. 7

```
H O P I T   C H A O T I C
A   R   R U   W   E   A
I R E L A N D   K N E A D
R   A   C   W     D
D U C H E S S   A L I B I
O   H   W   R   N   E
  M I N D R E A D I N G
H   N   U A   K   W
O U G H T   T A F F E T A
S   I       E   E   R
T H I E F   N O T E P A D
E   T   U A   C E   E
D E V E L O P   H E R O N
```

No. 8

```
  C L A R I F Y   E T C H
I   Y   E I   I R   U
T A R   P A R E N T I N G
A   I   O   S F   B E
L U C A S   T U R N U P
I       E   T T   B
C A S H E W   S Q U E A L
S   C   S   U       O
  C H I S E L   E L B O W
D   O   I E   N R   D
R U L I N G O U T   A I R
O   A   G N   L I   Y
P E R K   V A R Y I N G
```

No. 9

```
R E C I P E   H A N G U P
E   U   O   F   L E   E
C A R   L E I C E S T E R
E   S   A   G     E   I
S H E E R   U N R A V E L
S     B   R   E   E
  N E V E R E N D I N G
    M A   I   H     I
C A B A R E T   A L I E N
A   A     O   N   R   V
B A R B E C U E D   A L I
E   G   W   T   E   T   T
R O O F E R   A D H E R E
```

No. 10

```
M   V   J   E   S   A   S
A N A T O M Y   L U N C H
T   N   I   E   E   N   U
C L O W N   S E A W E E D
H   U   I   Z       D
  S T A N D T H E P A C E
T   E     O     P   R
S I N G L E M I N D E D
U     A     E   R   U
N U R T U R E   E D I T S
A   I   N   A   D   T   A
M U S I C   S U L K I N G
I   K   H   E   E   F   E
```

No. 11

```
S   M D   D   A   S
P E A C O C K   R E L I C
I   G   R   A   E   A   A
N A N N Y   T R A I N E R
D   E     E E D     Y
L A S   D O W N F A L L
Y   I   E   I   U   A   S
  P A T E R N A L   M U M
T   P   S     E   E O
O A T M E A L   J A N E T
T   A   N   E   O T   H
A N K L E   T R A P E Z E
L   E D     N   D R
```

No. 12

```
A   O H   N   I   F
M I C K E Y   B A R T E R
U   C   L   A   P   C   U
S C U L P T U R E   H E M
E   P   L   T     P   P
D R I V E H O M E   S T Y
    E   S M   L   T
F I R   S T A T E L E S S
E     T   C   P   E
W O K   D R I F T W O O D
E   E U   C   O   N   A
S H R I E K   A R T I S T
T   R   L     S   T   E
```

No. 13

```
D E P   E   C T S
R E N E E   F O O L I S H
O   O R   F   O E   A
V E R T I G O   K A R E N
E   M   O R   E     E
  C O L D S T O R A G E
    U       O
  A S T O N I S H I N G
S   P   S I D   S
P A N D A   L O G B O O K
A   I Q   A   H   L   U
S U N B U R N   E M A I L
M   E E   D   R   S L
```

No. 14

```
P U R S U E   T A U R U S
  N   P   X   R   N   N
T S A R   T O E N A I L S
  T   A   R   A   I   I
N U P T I A L S   D O T E
  C     O   U   E
S K A T E R   R U D E L Y
    H   D   E     A
A B L E   I N C I T I N G
  E   A   N   H   U   T
F A S T L A N E   T E E M
  N   R   R   S   O   R
L O V E L Y   T H R O N E
```

No. 15

```
T I P S Y   O P P R E S S
  N   H I   U   I   L
I N T E R N E T   S E E P
  E   L C   T   E   N
G R O T T O   H I R E D
    E   M   E     E
B L U R   P E W   R A R E
  I     E   I   A
  F L E E T   N O V I C E
  T   M E   D   I   L
D O S E   N E U R O T I C
  F   L C   P   L   N
O F F I C E R   B I N G E
```

No. 16

```
O P T I M U M   C R A S H
  H   N   S   S   O   T
H O U S E H O L D W O R D
  N   I   E   E     O
C E N S O R E D   T O B Y
  Y   T     G   O   E
  S E R V I E T T E
  L   N   A     T   D
F O O T   N A T T E R E D
O     D   H   N   C
A F T E R A F A S H I O N
  A   R   L   N   A   D
S H I R T   S K I M M E D
```

No. 17

```
C O N S O L E D   A L P S
  D   K   I   O U   I
A D D I N G   G O B B L E
  S   H     E   L
B O Y C O T T S   R O O T
  N H   Y   E G   W
    D A R E D E V I L
  S   R   A   I   N B
W A L T   R E N D E R E D
  C   E       G     L
C H O R U S   R A I S I N
  E   E   O   E V   E
S T U D   B A D L Y O F F
```

No. 18

```
D E N Y   P A T I E N T S
  N   I   O   O A   A
R A R E S T   R A T I N G
  M   L   T   N E
T E N D   Y E A R N I N G
  L   E     D     A
S L I D E T R O M B O N E
  E     H     U     N
A D A P T I N G   S O Y A
    R   S   R   P   G
T H R I F T   A M A Z O N
  O   S   L   S S   A
S W E E T E N S   S I T E
```

No. 19

```
A D A M   S U S P E N S E
  E   I   H U   L E
S M U D G E   B R E A T H
  A   W   L Z   C
O N C E   F R E T T I N G
  D   E     R     E
P I C K O U T O F A H A T
  N     N     R R
E G G S H E L L   R I T A
    H   Q   O   A   H
G A T E A U   L E N T I L
  D   A   A   L   G N
U S E F U L L Y   E D G Y
```

No. 20

```
B E D S I T   S T A N C E
  A   H R   H   T   O
B R A I N I E R   T U B A
  L   N   V   U   I   B
D Y E D   I M B E C I L E
    I     A       E
  H I G H L I G H T E R
  A     E   I
A R M C H A I R   L A W N
  B   R   L   M   T   A
C O M A   F L A M I N G O
  U   T   I   N   N   E
G R E E C E   Y O G U R T
```

No. 21

```
R   W   A       C   D H
O V E R L A P   H E A D Y
A   A   L   A   E   N P
D A N   E X P E R T I S E
H   G   E   R   E
O Z O N E   R O Y A L T Y
G   P   W       L   I
S W E E T I E   O B E S E
  R   I   I   U     E
R E A R L I G H T   D U D
O   T   T   H   L   E I
S I E G E   T R A D E I N
Y   S   D       W D   G
```

No. 22

```
  S   S   G   A S   C
S T I T C H E S   N O R M
  A   E   E   L I   A
O B J E C T   E M P T Y
  L   P   T   E E   O
R E E L   O P P O S I N G
      E     D     I
E P I S O D E S   D U C T
  U     R   A E   O
L A S S O   I N S O L E
  P   I   O   L H   E
R I N G   P R O V O K E S
  T   N   Y   R W   N
```

No. 23

```
  E   C   T   O   G   A
F L O O D I N G   R I L E
  S   M   P   L O   L
D E T E S T   E D W A R D
    I   O     U   O
S P E N C E R   S P O U T
  O     D F     N
F L O O R   T O W A R D S
  L   R     R I
H U B C A P   M E D L E Y
  T   H   L U   I D
J E D I   A T L A N T I C
  S   D   Y   A G   T
```

No. 24

```
  L   R Q     T H
M I N O G U E   S H E A R
  B   C   I   P E   R
D E S K   P A R S N I P S
  L   P     A     I
    L O N D O N   L O S S
  D   O   E   C A   T
O R A L   C R E A M Y
  A     A   P   P
G U I D E D O G   P A L E
  G   I   E   R O   A
C H E A T   D I S S E N T
  T   Z   M   T     B
```

No. 25

```
  D A L M A T I A N S
  M   A   E   S P   Y
S O A P S   M I S S I L E
H   Z   C   P   E N   L
O V E R A W E   T I D A L
E       R   R   R     R
    I N A B A D W A Y
  M       M   O     H
R E P A Y   E A R L O B E
O   O   O   N   K N   R
B O U Q U E T   S L I D E
E   N   R   A   H   O
  D I S P L A Y I N G
```

No. 26

```
F A N T A S Y   E Q U I P
U   A   T   G   U   C
S T O D G Y   E R A S E R
H   P   E   S   I   B
R O T O R   S T I L T O N
R   L   C   U       X
  R E L A Y R A C E
S       R   E   U   T
S T E W A R D   A T L A S
A   I   I   A   I   V
B R I D G E   S A C K E D
C   E   D   I   L   R
C H A R M   P A G E A N T
```

No. 27

```
  U D D E R   S W I L L
B   E   L   I   A   W
E A S T E R   F L O W E R
R   E   C   P D F   O
T U R N T O A C C O U N T
H   T   R   L A L   E
    D I C T A T E
S   B   C   R S C   J
T R A N S P O R T C A F E
U   R   H   W R R   W
D E R M O T   N I B B L E
Y   E   C   K   O   L
  B L O K E   B E I N G
```

No. 28

```
  S   A   L E O   A   J
S C A R C E   V A L U E D
  R   A   V   E   P   T
F E E B L E   R E A L L Y
  A   I   L   A   C   A
S M E A R C A M P A I G N
A       R   B       H
T E A R T O R I B B O N S
R   A   S   T   A   U
C R I S I S   I G N O R E
I   H   I   O   K   S
I N T E R N   U N E V E N
G   R   G A S   R   D
```

No. 29

```
    F   B   L   S
  P A N O R A M I C
R   C   T   P G L
S E X I S T   T O N S I L
H   A   L O O   A   M
G O A L I E   P I L F E R
U   O       N   G
A S Y L U M   I N J U R E
I   A   O W N   U   E
A N S W E R   C A L L E R
G   S   B   A   I   N
  M O V I E S T A R
  N   D   E   N
```

No. 30

```
  C A S   S   A   N
T H R U S T   H E L P E D
  R   S   A   E   E L
P O R T U G A L   C A L L
  M   R   L       I
D E M I   W R I N K L E S
  A   H   N   A
S T I N G I N G   T H I N
  H   S   E   N
S I L L   T R I U M P H S
  R   O   L   T O A
S T A R V E   E A S I L Y
  Y   D   D M   S E
```

No. 31

```
  G   L R C   S   N
H O U S E Y H O U S E Y
O   N   C   E   R A
H U N G R Y   F I G H T
L   C       I
P I T F A L L S   C L U B
  S O E   T   A N
C H A R   S P O T L E S S
  E       P       P
  S N A G S   P A T R O N
  O   R   H A R   I
S W I M M I N G P O O L
  N   S   A E T   T
```

No. 32

```
M U S E U M   I N F E S T
  N   X   A   C   O   L
N A R C I S S I   C H I P
  P   I   S E   A   N
S P O T   E A R P L U G S
  R   E   U       Y
V E N D O R   B A R L O W
  C       U   O   U
A I R T I G H T   O G R E
  A   O   U   T S   H
S T O W   A D O P T I O N
  E   E R   N   E   O
A D D L E D   S T R O K E
```

SOLUTIONS

No. 33

```
  A P   S E C   M
A L K A L I   D A Y O U T
  L I   E G C   F
F E N D   S K I L L E T S
  G   T   N O   I
R E A R R A N G I N G
  D E       I   B
    S C R A T C H C A R D
  A   R   V O   O
A N G E L I N A   C A S T
  N   A   A R O N
L O O T E R   S A N D A L
  Y E   Y E   E N
```

No. 34

```
  A E F   S P E
S U G G E S T I O N S
  H G A   Y E T
M O T H E R   L E T H A L
  R E E   E   T
R E W A R D E D   B R E D
  D       L
A S K S   R O C K E T E D
  H   E   H E   N
R I T U A L   O R P H A N
  F S A   P I   M
T W E N T Y P E N C E
  Y R E   Y G   L
```

No. 35

```
  S U M M E R H O U S E
S   P I A   X W U
O B S E S S I V E N E S S
  R   T D N   E I
R E F O R M E R   S T U N
  Y E U D   C E   G
  P A U S E   J O I N T
  R T T I   A E   C
A C H E   S M O U L D E R
  B E Y   P T   E
B E R M U D A S H O R T S
  I E L   C O U   S
  A D V E N T U R I N G
```

No. 36

```
  C A L C U L A T O R S
N C   A A E   U E
E G O   S I G N A L B O X
  R R U O   T D T
V I N D A L O O   R O A R
  E   L N E W   A
C A V I T Y   S A T N A V
  E   E Y G R   A
N O T E   L E A P F R O G
  T E S   R I E
R E R E L E A S E   S U N
  E A U R   C E T
  I N G R E D I E N T S
```

No. 37

```
S O L V E   A U C T I O N
T A X   S   H N U
I N D E P T H   A S K E D
F Y A   T   I
L O B S T E R   T H E F T
E I   O   E N Y
  I R I S M U R D O C H
B D T G   O H
I S S U E   E N R O U T E
G   F   I N A
T I A R A   J U P I T E R
O P N A   U E T
P R E M I U M   P A R T Y
```

No. 38

```
C O N S U M E   R O S E
T U W O   I R V
H E N   E X T E N S I V E
R C E O T   G R
I N E P T   R E H E A T
V T   E   M P
E M P L O Y   U L R I K A
D R O   O P
  B A R T O N   N A S T Y
L I H O G   A R
I N S P E C T O R   L O U
A E D C U   S S
M A D E   S H I N P A D
```

No. 39

```
I M P O R T   A C C E N T
N R E B   A A A
C O O   C O L O N I S T S
O U A O   T T
M O D E L   O B S C E N E
E   L D E R
  A C H I E V E M E N T
L N E   I A
T W I N G E S   C A D E T
E M   S O I O
A L A R M B E L L   S O N
R T A L   O C C
S T E N C H   E N C O R E
```

No. 40

```
  A S S   C S A
F O U N T A I N P E N
  F B R   T A G
S A L U T E   R A M B L E
  I R E U   I
T R I B U T E S   D E A R
  I       E
I S L A   M A D E S U R E
  N   I I O E
P E L V I S   V A L L E Y
  A O C   I A V
K I T C H E N E T T E
  Y E A   G E S
```

SOLUTIONS

No. 41

```
A B P . . B U W . . .
T O L D O F F . R A N C H
H E . S . O . I . I . E
E S S A Y . R E G A T T A
I . S . S . S . H . . T
S O Y . R O T A T I N G .
T . O . E . A . A . U .
. P U M P I R O N . T A T
D . . A . T . . I . T .
E N S U I T E . N O O S E
R . L . R . R . E . N . R
B R A V E . S E A W A L L
Y . M . D . . R . L . Y
```

No. 42

```
S . L . T . . R H . S
T H E S I S . M A K E U P
A . O . D . P . N . A . I
T I N K E R I N G . D O N A
U . A . M . R . . . . A
S P R E A D O U T . P A L
. D . . R . U . I . R
B O O . K E E P C L E A R
R . . . T . K . C . O
E A R . O N T H E R O A D
A . A . W . E . T . O
C H I L L Y . R E C K O N
H . D . S . . D . S . T
```

No. 43

```
G . V B . S . C A . B
E V I T A . N E U T R A L
T . R . Z . A . C . E . E
O U T B A C K . K O A L A
N . U . A . E . O . . K
. C O R R E S P O N D S
. . U . . . . . . E
. A S K I N G P R I C E
S . . O . A . O . L . C
T O W E D . T O B L A M E
A . I . I . H . B . R . A
I M M E N S E . E V E N S
D . P . E . R . R . S . E
```

No. 44

```
F O S S I L . P R E P A Y
. R . A . E . I . V . C
S L A B . A L L N I G H T
. A . R . V . O . C . E
I N T E R E S T . T I D E
D . . S . S . E
C O R S E T . L A D D E R
. T . . A . I . . . N
T A X I . N E C K L A C E
. L . M . D . E . O . L
S O L U T I O N . D O O R
N . L . N . C . G . S
A G E I N G . E L E V E N
```

No. 45

```
O S C A R . A D D R E S S
. I . B . H . I . O . O
R E I S S U E S . B O A R
. V . C . N . I . O . N
B E L O N G . N O T E D
. N . E . F . . S
H A N D . R Y E . C H O P
I . . S . C . O
R O A S T . T R U A N T
P . L . R . I . N . A
J O L T . I N N O T I M E
R . O . K . G . E . E
S T U N N E D . C R U D E
```

No. 46

```
S A N D P I T . A D O P T
. F . A . M . C . Y . O
D R U M M A J O R E T T E
. A . P . G . T . . A
M I S S P E L T . O A T H
. D . Q . . O . V . O
. G U A R A N T E E
. A . I . A . . R . U
S N U B . P I E R C I N G
. D . . I . E . O . S
G R O U N D B R E A K E R
E . S . S . I . T . E
D A T E D . T E A S I N G
```

No. 47

```
R A V E N O U S . M E W S
. R . M . F . I . A . R
S C R U F F . R U D D E R
. H . . L . E . A
T E A C L O T H . M O T H
. D . L . A . A . O . H
. R E D D E N I N G
. M . R . E . D . E . E
R U N G . D E L A Y I N G
. S . Y . . E . . C
S C A M P I . B A M B O O
. L . E . T . A . O . D
V E I N . S T R A P P E D
```

No. 48

```
O M I T . U N D E R F E D
. E . R . N . I . U . V
S C R I M P . S E R V E D
. H . U . I . A . A
F A R M . N O B I L I T Y
. N . P . . L . . A
P I G H E A D E D N E S S
. S . . V . . E . T
I M P E R I L S . I D E A
. A . A . C . T . L
D R Y R O T . A S H L E Y
. A . O . L . E . S
I N T H E R E D . R I S E
```

SOLUTIONS

No. 49

```
HEEL   BACKDROP
A  I   L    U  I  N
ESCAPE   REGRET
Y  I    S   R  I
EGGS   SWATTING
O  O    N       E
MIDNIGHTFEAST
N    H    Q  T
AGUILERA   UGLY
   N  R   L  A  I
ATTACK   INTENT
O  P    I  A  O  G
MEETINGS   RUSH
```

No. 50

```
CHOOSE   MODIFY
O  P  P   I  E  O
ALTERING   CORD
L  N   S   H  O  S
TYRA   OUTBREAK
   I   D       L
 GARDENGNOME
W     R   C
SYLLABLE   TACT
N  U   U  N  O  O
KEEN   SCABBARD
T  G   H  D  E  G
CHEEKY   EARWIG
```

No. 51

```
C  A  B    W  E  E
HYGIENE   ESSEX
E  E   L  A  A   I
RED   FORASTART
U     R   T  E  P
BUDDY   HELPING
I  I   S     N  U
CERAMIC   CIGAR
   E  U  R  A    G
SECATEURS   DEL
O  T   T  S  K  O  I
SUEDE   TREASON
O  D   R    T  H  G
```

No. 52

```
T  S  G  S  B   A
THROWOUT   EURO
R  M   B   I  A  C
GENEVA   NORTH
A  R   C  G     E
ODDS   KEYBOARD
   E       P
SCOTLAND   PAWN
A   T  E  O  A
SCRUB   ASSURE
U  U   E  D  I  P
BALM   SPLUTTER
L  P   T  Y  E  D
```

No. 53

```
   A  T  B  S  P  S
BLOWLAMP   RICH
S  E   B  U  U  H
BOUNTY   DANCER
   T  S   E   M
ACRYLIC   ADMIT
O    T  N    N
INLAW   BOROUGH
C  C   M  N
BEATEN   AVENUE
D  I   E  D  D  S
BEAN   WRIGGLES
D  G   T  C  E  D
```

No. 54

```
F  S  P    D  E
MINIBUS   PIANO
N  C   M  S  S  V
LARK   PANICKED
L  N   E     L
 SEETHE   COOL
R  S   O  Z  O  P
PEGS   PRYING
V   D   C  R
DIVEBOMB   ROAD
V  A   G  O  E  L
BELCH   HOSTILE
D  H    K  E  Y
```

No. 55

```
 REFUNDABLE
   R  N   I  R  D  B
HURON   SPANIEL
A  E   E  C  S  T  U
UNDERGO   SPINE
L    V  U     O
 GREENHORN
A    T  U    S
JAMES   SETSAIL
O  B   I   C  L  I
INLIMBO   AWARD
N  E   O  R  S  R
 DINNERTIME
```

No. 56

```
CANVASS   AMONG
L  E   T  P  E   I
FIERCE   OUTING
G  D   W  S  A  E
CHOIR   ISOLATE
T  C   F  E     Y
 STYLISHLY
P    A  S  O  S
FANNING   EVICT
G  A   N  C  A  O
COOKIE   AUBURN
D  E   L  M  L  E
CARDS   VENEERS
```

SOLUTIONS

No. 57

```
  F A T A L   S M A L L
Y   T   G   I   O   G
U P T U R N   E X P O S E
C   E   E   S   E   S
C O N T E N T E D N E S S
A   D   T   O   M   N   E
    D O O R M A T
E   S   D   A   R   M   A
R U N R I N G S R O U N D
U   I   F   E   I   R   O
  P U T O F F   L A R D E R
T   C   E   G   E   E
  W H I R R   K E R R Y
```

No. 58

```
  S   B   C U R   F   L
T H R E S H   E L O P E D
  R   A   A   L   R   N
  P I N C E R   A R M I N G
  M   O   A   T   A   O
S P I N E C H I L L I N G
I   T   O   O   O
T O N G U E I N C H E E K
  U   R   R   S   I   Y
S T R O L L   H O L M E S
  L   U   E   I   A   L
T E N N I S   P A R C E L
  T   D   S O S   Y   T
```

No. 59

```
    K   S W M
  D U S T C O V E R
  S   N   O   N   D
S T A G D O   L O I T E R
  O   F   G E L   A   V
A R O U S E   Y E L L O W
  E   U   Y   U
P R I V E T   R E T I R E
  O   E   A X E   A   I
H O U R L Y   L I N I N G
  M   S   L   I K   G
    O U T O F S T E P
    S   R   H   R
```

No. 60

```
  C   L   S T C   A
H E A D T E A C H E R
  I   N   R   B   U   R
S L U D G E   L I M P E T
  L   S   A   E   S
D I P L O M A T   D A T A
  I           I
J U M P   E X P A N D E D
N   S   A   E   N
R E M A R K   R I D D L E
A   T   I   T   O   I
S T O R M C L O U D S
E   M   O   Y   T   T
```

No. 61

```
  M   A   O W F   P
A B N O R M A L L O A D
G   O   G   R   E   I
V I E N N A   D I X O N
C       N       I
C I R C U I T S   B A N G
A   A   S   P   L   E
K N O T   T A R G E T E D
  T           A   D
A I R E D   Y E A R L Y
F   A   A   I   G   E
T A B L E M A N N E R S
R   L   P   G   S   S
```

No. 62

```
P H O B I A   R A P A C E
  O   A   P   I   E   A
S U F F E R E D   T I L T
  S   F   I   E   R   E
V E I L   C U R T A I N S
  B   E   O       D
C R E D I T   S E E S A W
  E       U   N   R
H A D A B A L L   L I M B
  K   R   T   T   A   O
D I G S   S C A R R I N G
  N   O   E   N   G   T
A G E N D A   A R E T H A
```

No. 63

```
  B   D   E   P   I   A
B I K I N I   O W N I N G
  F   E   T   N   C   G
L O U D   H E C K L E R S
  C   E   H   I   Y
G A T H E R R O U N D
  L   U       E   T
    F L A K Y P A S T R Y
  B   A   E   I       E
C A S H M E R E   R E A P
K   O   P   R   Y   C
D E M O T E   C R A D L E
R   P   R   E   N   E
```

No. 64

```
  S   A   Z   L P   B
T E R M I N O L O G Y
  Y   M   N   U   U   P
A L B I O N   N O R M A L
  E   N   I   G       S
E S C A L A T E   P O S T
  R           H
S C A M   C O N C O C T S
  R   O   E   N   A
R E D I A L   P L E D G E
  E   R   L   H   B   G
P R O F I T E R O L E
  Y   N   E   W X   D
```

No. 65

```
HALFBROTHER
TAPERECORDING
REBELLED PEEL
SAUNA MUSTY
ROTA OINTMENT
SAFETYDEPOSIT
ILLMANNERED
```

No. 66

```
CURIOSITIES
TOT JAREDLETO
TOLERANT LARA
OUTSET HECTIC
COPY AMERICAN
PROSECUTE ILL
NATURESTUDY
```

No. 67

```
CUSHY UNTRIED
ABANDON DAVID
UNBOLTS LILAC
HALFHEARTED
ADDER PIRANHA
HELLO HOLDALL
LIPREAD CATTY
```

No. 68

```
EMBASSY ACRE
TOO TERMINALS
MAYBE EYELID
LEAGUE HELENA
CENSUS SARAH
CHILDCARE APT
DAYS PRESUME
```

No. 69

```
ASSENT FLIGHT
TWO RESISTING
THERE ADAPTOR
ATFIRSTHAND
STETSON ERECT
INKBOTTLE TAR
KIDNEY ASTRAY
```

No. 70

```
PRIMATE FAULT
WATER PRIVATE
UNECONOMICAL
HANDKERCHIEF
BACKROW NEIGH
ROSIE PREVENT
```

No. 71

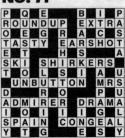

```
ROUNDUP EXTRA
TASTY EARSHOT
SKI SHIRKERS
UNBUTTON MRS
ADMIRER DRAMA
SPAIN CONGEAL
```

No. 72

```
ONEDAY MORTAR
WRONGDOER BOY
NETPROFIT FOR
CAD THEMEPARK
UHT STAYEDPUT
BABBLE PETROL
```

SOLUTIONS

No. 73

```
D S T A S S C
ITALY SHAMPOO
R T R P F U H
TSUNAMI AGREE
Y R N R R N
 BATTLEFIELD
 T I
 SEASICKNESS
S H R E T E
ORDER AMERICA
A E O T D N T
PICTURE EAGLE
Y K D R D S N
```

No. 74

```
AMUSED SPLASH
I A O T E T
GRIN CHARADES
A T U N R E
UNHARMED NULL
D E I E
RATRUN NODOFF
E T G I
ABET ADOPTING
R R T R O A
PACIFIED NINE
V A O E E C
POLLEN REDEEM
```

No. 75

```
S P M S P A
CARSICKNESS
R E R A E S
LESSER TURNUP
E S O E M
ENQUIRED DREW
R E
OBOE VILLAINS
O A I D I
PICNIC QUENCH
L E A U N O
ELECTRICEEL
D D E D D E
```

No. 76

```
NATURAL WALES
I N L T L V
DROPLIKEFLIES
B O E N N
DEEPENED FOUR
D U E L P
 FLOWERPOT
F A A O F
BLUR LITERARY
E L B S I
NEXTTONOTHING
C A W N O G
WEANS SEAWEED
```

No. 77

```
PROBABLY HATE
E A U E A R
LAUREL SKIVER
R L R N
DEFENDER INCH
D M O E N H
 ZIGZAGGED
C G E I S K
TOUR DOMESTIC
L A E M
PORTER NARROW
N E A T E N
DYED FASTFOOD
```

No. 78

```
XMAS NOBLEMAN
U T U I D G
ASCEND CLIPON
H P G Y T
IRIS EXCUSING
O O L U
COUNTTHEHOURS
M R R S
USHERING BLED
A P R I M
TASSEL ACTUAL
L E E N A I
DEPLETED LIDO
```

No. 79

```
TWEE GROOMING
E Y A I O H
MADEUP LATEST
K L E L E
FLEA DRAWLING
I S M O
INTHEPIPELINE
G O I E
ISOLATES BONO
I S U E T
WARMTH PERMIT
R B O E T T
IMPOSTOR YOYO
```

No. 80

```
ICICLE AFFECT
H L X S E A
RELEVANT TUBA
A A M O C B
SPIN PUNCHBAG
E L G
 FORGETTABLE
L O L
PACKEDUP EASY
V E O S N H
COMA DWINDLED
U N G D E E
GROUSE EUROPE
```

SOLUTIONS

No. 81

```
O   A   F       H   D   H
BERMUDA     ALICE
J   I   N   C   G   L   R
ERA RECOGNISE
C       U   O   I   G
TAKEN   MYSTERY
E   I       P       N   I
DILEMMA     UNTIE
    L   A   N   R       L
REJIGGING   BID
A   O   N   S   E   A   I
THYME   TENSION
E   S   T       T   T   G
```

No. 82

```
    U   O   D   I   D   S
SNIPPETS    IDLE
D   T   V   S   V   O
DOMINO  USEUP
N   O   U   E       E
SEAN    REDHEADS
    A       A
EYELINER    RODE
O       A   E   N   A
GRUMP   WHISKY
U   R   K   A   N   O
DRUG    IRRIGATE
T   E   N   D   S   A
```

No. 83

```
    S   O   A   S   C   M
STUNTMAN    HOOD
    Y   C   M   A   A   T
PEDALO  GOSLOW
    L   N       E   R
IDYLLIC     TRUCE
E       A   C       A
SCOWL   VENDORS
A   I       R   E
SNATCH  TAVERN
T   H   Y   A   I   I
DEMI    PLIMSOLL
R   N   E   N   E   E
```

No. 84

```
    F   P   A       L   R
ELLIPSE     NEWER
O   C   I   W   N   R
FOLK    ACIDDROP
D   L   N       U
    MIRREN  KATE
I   N   U   E   N   E
SNOG    MARROW
S   B       C   C
BUNGALOW    KNOW
L   U   E   A   O   N
YIELD   DIVULGE
N   L   T   T   A
```

No. 85

```
    SIDEEFFECT
    N   Y   U   L   E   C
FABLE   NETBALL
O   O   T   N   O   C   U
ANXIETY NOONE
L       S   P       S
    BUTTERFLY
    E       C   O       T
PULSE   UNREADY
U   O   B   L   M   M   P
RAVIOLI USAGE
R   E   N   A   L   Z
    DAYDREAMED
```

No. 86

```
SUBJECT EVENT
N   U   O   U   O   E
STOKED  NUTMEG
R   E   E   S   E   D
TUBBY   STERILE
E   O   P   U       E
    EXTRACTOR
B       O   K   R   S
CONSULT HATCH
G   E   O   T   N   A
COLEEN  REGARD
T   D   G   E   E   E
KANYE   SEASIDE
```

No. 87

```
    BRUCE   GNOME
S   E   O       A   E   C
INVENT  POSTER
X   E   T   S   M   H   O
TEARASTRIPOFF
Y   L   C   A   C   D   T
    ETERNAL
S   C   L   T   M   D   S
WHITEELEPHANT
E   N   N   E   B   I   A
EVENSO  KENNEL
T   M   E       L   T   L
    MARSH   LLOYD
```

No. 88

```
    D   R   FEW O   A
GEMINI  IMPISH
G   T   N   L   P   W
TROUPE  LOOTER
E   A   T   O   S   L
MEALSONWHEELS
A       O   P       I
PARROTFASHION
N   E   H   T   A   F
STATIC  THRIFT
L   A   O   E   D   E
HELIUM  RULING
R   L   BEN Y   D
```

366

No. 89

```
    R C E A
   REFURNISH
 G F D R S R
BYROAD ALEVEL
 M R LOG S P
SKIMPY EASILY
 H I   I A
FARMER GLITCH
 N E EVA N I
GALLOP RISING
 S O A L T G
  ADDITIVES
  Y R C P
```

No. 90

```
 S C S P O F
SACHET RAGGED
 L O O R T
NARROWED EDIT
 M U U S
PIPS BACKACHE
 E O E I
PRESUMES RULE
 E B F E
ACTS SURGICAL
 I T I U E D
SPOILT BALLET
 E R E Y D R
```

No. 91

```
 D S G Q S R
 INTERRUPTION
 N U E I R S
DOWNEY PRESS
 S N S S
WARINESS SOME
 U N S E E O
FRET SCALDING
 H F G
 WHEEL RATION
 E W A O U O
ASSASSINATES
 T Y T T U E
```

No. 92

```
ALWAYS RARITY
 E C T E O E
BACTERIA MIME
 R R O C E P
KNEE POTHOLER
 E S P R
TRASHY ORDEAL
 D S I M
PRECINCT ALEX
 I E E R G N
EVIL EMIGRATE
 E L D C A A
BROODY HOMELY
```

No. 93

```
 I S C S M C
ALBINO UNABLE
 L L O D G A
MILL GOODNESS
 C A K E S
DISTINGUISH
 T H I S
 SEARCHPARTY
 C R O A Y
FROMATOZ COLD
 A A A A I
SCULPT REVISE
 K S E D E H
```

No. 94

```
 A F R C F E
 PARLOURMAID
 P U N O W W
REGION CONMAN
 A T I U R
DRIFTERS RIDE
 U O
IDOL TEMPLATE
 I R A L I
ANGORA REEVES
 G L N I D D
HALFCENTURY
 Y Y E E P E
```

No. 95

```
 CERTIFICATE
P A U R O A B
INTERNATIONAL
L N M N G A
LOITERED TEAM
S N D D S R E
 AGAIN RESIN
S E N H A N U
TENT SOURNESS
O E L T C I
CARRIEDTHECAN
K A M O M O G
 ELBOWGREASE
```

No. 96

```
 CHOCKABLOCK
N E A U A L M
END SENSITIVE
W G H T D M R
BREADBIN TALC
O E E R T I
RECESS CEREAL
N H K D D E
BEEF FIELDERS
A E R V I R S
BARTERING OWL
Y I N N H D Y
 SOFTCENTRED
```

SOLUTIONS

No. 97

```
B O A S T   R E N E W A L
O   L O   A   O E   I
W A L K W A Y   S T E A K
I   A   E       E   E
N A T A L I E   B R A W L
G   O     V   A L   Y
  K N O C K I N G O U T
A   C   A   T     M   E
S T E E P   A U C T I O N
L   I       R     N   I
E X P A T   H E A D I N G
E   T A   E   I   U   M
P R O W L E R   G E M M A
```

No. 98

```
  T U R R E T S   R O A R
E   N   I R   K   V   I
D A D   N E E D I N E S S
U   E   G   N R R   K
C H R I S   D I S M A Y
A   I       T   L   E
T R E A D S   R E F L E X
E   Y   E     N     T
  B E D S I T   D I V E R
K   S E   W   U   I   E
I S O L A T I O N   G E M
E   R   T S   S   I   E
V E E R   S T A T E L Y
```

No. 99

```
T R I L B Y   Q U I R K Y
E   D   R A   S E   E
A L I   O R C H E S T R A
B   O   A   C   R   R
A C T E D   E X P L A I N
G   B   P   A   I
  A D V E N T U R I N G
  R   A A   T       C
B R O S N A N   R I V A L
E   P   C   I   I   U
A P P R E H E N D   S A M
C   E   E S   G   O   S
H E R A L D   N E A R B Y
```

No. 100

```
V   M   V   E C F   I
I N I T I A L   L I E I N
N   S C   L   I T   S
Y A C H T   E N C H A N T
L   O   I   H     U
  S U M M E R S E A S O N
L   N   I     U   T
E A T H U M B L E P I E
A   N     X   T   R
T O Y S H O P   H E A V E
H   O U   A   A   B   I
E A G E R   Y U L E L O G
R   A T S   E   Y N
```

No. 101

```
C   N   E     H G   K
H O O D L U M   E L L E N
E   G   S O   D   U   E
D R O N E   D I G I T A L
D   A   E   E   T   T
A I R   B A R C H A R T
R   E O   N O   E   A
  M A T U R I N G   B I N
A   Q   S     O   A
S T I M U L I   Y O U N G
K   C   E   N   E   R
E X E R T   G R A N D P A
W   D S     R   S   M
```

No. 102

```
S   B   D     M   M   A
H E A V E N   R E M A I N
A   G C D   E   S   I
D O U B L E A C T   K I M
O   E   A S       A
W A T E R S H E D   N I L
    T   E B   I U
I K E   S P O N S O R E D
N       A H   T   R
S A D   P E R S E C U T E
E   A E   D   D R   A
C Y M B A L   M U S E U M
T   N L     P   D T
```

No. 103

```
H   D   R   B T   L   M
I B I Z A   I M A G I N E
P   S   B   N   R N   S
P A C K I N G   G R O S S
O   A   E   E   E   Y
  I R I S H S E T T E R
    D         N
  A S S E R T I V E L Y
L   N   I   I A     A
U N L E T   C H E E R E D
N   I   I   K W   G A
C O N T R O L   E Y E U P
H   E   E E   R   D   T
```

No. 104

```
P U R S U E   F I N A L E
  N   C X   U   O   A
T E R I   C O L L E C T S
  A   F E   L   N   I
T R A I N S E T   T I N Y
  T     S   O R
C H E R U B   T O Y B O Y
  U   A H       B
S C A N   G R E A T E S T
  H   I G   B   R   C
A L A N C A R R   A G E D
  O   T   G   I   W   N
R E M O T E   M I L L E R
```

368

No. 105

```
W A S T E   A T A P U S H
V   O   G     E   E   K
T E A S P O O N   T R I P
  R   P   R   N   A   T
S T R A N D   I N L E T
  R   O     S       L
M O P E   N I P   J E E R
  R   R   L   A
  L L A M A   A R C A D E
  A   N   M   Y   U   U
S N U G   S N E E Z I N G
  D   E   A   R   Z   C
V O L L E Y S   F I V E R
```

No. 106

```
P A S S I O N   P R O B E
  B   W   W   W   U   U
M O T I O N P I C T U R E
  A   N   E   L     R
B R I G A D E S   S W O T
  D   B     O   O   W
    R O U T I N E L Y
  M   A   A     D   S
C A R T   R U F F I A N S
  K     T   U   E   A
G E N E R A L S T R I K E
  D   W   N   S   O   E
J O K E R   G Y M N A S T
```

No. 107

```
B A G P I P E R   S A S H
  N   R   O   U   T   E
A C R O S S   N E A T E N
  H   S     M   I
C O N C R E T E   P O N D
  R   H   S   V   E   G
    H A T S T A N D S
  H   R   E   L   E   J
G I L L   S Q U A S H E S
  G   O     A       T
G H E T T O   T O P P L E
  E   T   I   E   U   A
T R U E   L A D Y G A G A
```

No. 108

```
M A L E   F O R T R E S S
  C   L   A   U   E   K
E C L A I R   P O P E Y E
  O   S   C   T   E
G R I T   E Q U A L I T Y
  D   I   R       H
D I S C O N N E C T I O N
  O   O     R   U   U
I N C L I N E D   E A S T
    E   D   R   A   A
A U P A I R   I N T E N T
  M   R   I   F   E   D
P A I N T P O T   D U S K
```

No. 109

```
T O R N   E M B A R K E D
  U   A   G   I   M
S T A R R Y   G E N I U S
  G   R   P   O   S
S O Y A   T A T T E R E D
  I   T     E       N
I N D E P E N D E N T L Y
  G   V       O   A
E S C A P I N G   T I R E
    D   D   L   H   G
R E F U S E   O R I G I N
  L   L   N   S   N   N
I M I T A T E S   G A G A
```

No. 110

```
C H A C H A   E N T I C E
  A   L   B   L   A   H
G R U E S O M E   B E A T
  S   A   L   C   L   R
C H I N   I N T R E P I D
      S   S       S   T
    M E E T H A L F W A Y
  A       O   A
C L O S E T E D   R A I D
  A   H   H   G   R   G
T R I O   I N I T I A L S
  I   C   R   N   O   O
P A C K E D   G O R D O N
```

No. 111

```
M   G   E     G   I   T
A Q U A T I C   A R G U E
N   L   C   O   T   N   N
E L F   H O U S E H O L D
A     E   N   A   R
T I R E D   C O U R A G E
E   U   I       N   X
R A D I C A L   T O T U P
  E   U   L   U     O
M O N S T R O U S   J A R
I   E   L   R   S   U   T
T A S T E   S P L U R G E
T   S   T       E   Y   R
```

No. 112

```
M   W   B   S   G   T
B I G A M I S T   U N I T
D   V   S   A   R   N
A D V E R T   Y O U R S
  A   R   R E       E
T Y N E   O D D B A L L S
    R           D
C O N S I D E R   L A I R
  N   A   E   I   N
V E N O M   A M B U S H
  I   O   A   S   B   U
Z E R O   G E O M E T R Y
  W   K   E   N   D   E
```

SOLUTIONS

No. 113

```
  S   A   T   A   F U
S T I F F E N S   L I N T
  U   T   S   K U   S
O D D E S T   S L E U T H
  R   I       N   E
P R E S E N T   S T R A Y
  E       G G       D
J U D G E   W A Y L A Y S
  S   A       R   A
P A M P E R   B I G B E N
  B   I   O   A   O   X
A L A N   M A G N O L I A
  E   G   E   E   N   T
```

No. 114

```
  P   H   K       L   R
C R O O K E D   C A M E L
  O   L   Y   P   S   C
D O D O   S N A P S H O T
  F   G       U   U
    D R E A M S   W A N D
  S   A   L   E   R   T
I T E M   I N D I A N
  A       G       N   P
P R E A C H E R   G O R Y
  C   C   T   A   L   U
C H I N A   I N F E R N O
  Y   E   G   S   E
```

No. 115

```
  S H O E P O L I S H   E
  A   A   N   D   E   G
P A L E R   T O E N A I L
O   V   L   H   A   L U
O N E T I M E   L I T R E
L   E   C       H
    A I R W O R T H Y   T
  N       N   H       T
M A G I C   T R E M B L E
A   E   H   R   R   O E
S U L T A N A   M E G A N
S   I   R   A   U
  C A N D Y F L O S S
```

No. 116

```
A N I S T O N   A S S E T
  A   P   A   U E Y   Y
A T R E S T   M A I L E D
  I   C   H   P   Z   L
T O P I C   U T T E R E D
  N   A   B E       T
    B L U E B E R R Y
  C   R   N   O   R
M A D O N N A   E S S E X
  R   R   A   A   E   H
L E D G E R   B O T H E R
  E   A   D   L   T   A
T R U N K   S E V E N T Y
```

No. 117

```
  I R A T E   E N E M Y
P   E   R   O   A   H
L E T T E R   S T E R E O
U   I   A   C O   I   N
C H R I S T I A N B A L E
K   E   U   R   Y H   Y
    P R E C O O K
S   P   E   U   U S   R
M O U N T A I N R A N G E
E   R   R   T   L I   F
L A P T O P   P I M P L E
L   L   V       F   E R
  B E R E T   P E R R Y
```

No. 118

```
  B   D   CUT   S   V
T U X E D O   I T A L I C
  R   N   N   P   T S
B E A T I T   T E N N I S
  A   A   A   H   A O
P U B L I C S E R V A N T
A       T   B       A
L E A V E S T A N D I N G
  X   E   P   L   I I
F I A S C O   A D V I C E
  T   T   R   N   E K
S E C R E T   C U R S E D
  D   Y   SHE   T   L
```

No. 119

```
      S   T E   A
    R E A R R A N G E
  F   D   E   S E   D
A U B U R N   T A I L O R
  L   C   DOE   N   W
S L E E P Y   R E G E N T
  C   E       A   U
C R U F T S   E R R I N G
  E   E   COX   E   D
S A H A R A   T E M P E R
  M   R   M   R A   R
  K N A P S A C K S
      E   I S   E
```

No. 120

```
  F   B   T   C   T A
Y E A R L Y   A S S I S T
  M   A   R   P   A S
D A R K N E S S   R A I L
  L   E       U       G
Y E L P   A L L E G I N G
  A   L   E   O
G O N D O L A S   O U C H
  L   O       D   H
V I E W   C O M E D I A N
  V   E   A   U   E R
C E M E N T   S H A G G Y
  R   P   E   K   L E
```

No. 121

```
  N S H   B O   N
A T T H E M E R C Y O F
  I   E A   T C   S
F L A W E D   A B U S E
  F   L     P
D I A G R A M S   A L P S
  L   O   M E N   A
F E T E   P L A N T I N G
  A     T     T
  I S S U E   B E L F R Y
  S   Y   U E   E   I
U P Y O U R S L E E V E
  Y   N   O T   R   S
```

No. 122

```
A B A C U S   B I T C H Y
  R   A A   A   O   E
V I B R A T E S   W A R S
  T   T I   T E   E
I N T O   S T E P D O W N
  E   O F       E
S Y D N E Y   M I R A G E
  S       I   E   O
S P A C E M A N   C R A G
  E   R E   D I   G
D A M E   A L S A T I A N
  R   P N   E A   I
A S C E N T   T A L E N T
```

No. 123

```
  S D   T   P   G W
S T R I K E   E R A S E R
  R   S   A   L   T E
J O S H   S O M E H O P E
  K     E E   E S
T E M P E R A T U R E
  D   O       U U
  G I V E T H E P U S H
  E   S   X   O
O N E O R T W O   O W L S
  R   N   E T   I E
S O L E M N   E N L I S T
  L   D   D R   Y S
```

No. 124

```
  D   A M S   B E
  R E S P I R A T I O N
  A   S D   F K D
A G R E E D   E Y E L I D
  O   M   L T   N
S N O B B E R Y   S A G E
  L         T
S W A Y   C O S T U M E S
  A     A   U M X
A S Y L U M   G O B A C K
  H   A E   A L   I
  U N D E R A R R E S T
  P   Y A   Y D   E
```

No. 125

```
  T H E R M O M E T E R
P   O E   P   C   M A
O N T E N T E R H O O K S
P     D   N   O T   K
P O C K E T E D   F I V E
Y   A R D   S O D
  C R E E P   S K U N K
G   P D   B   I A   S
O W E N   G A U N T L E T
O   N G   N H     A
U N T H R E A T E N I N G
T   E I   N A D   E
  P R I D E A N D J O Y
```

No. 126

```
  B A K E R S D O Z E N
D   N X   T U   M   F
O L D   C H R I S T I N A
U   E E   I T   N   L
B U S T L I N G   T E L L
L     L   G O N   E
E I T H E R   B U T T I N
C   W D   G T     A
R I O T   L O G C A B I N
O   S L   K A   E   G
S T O W A W A Y S   A X E
S   M V   R T   N   L
  P E N A L T Y S P O T
```

No. 127

```
D I G I T   A N A R C H Y
E   R U G   N O   I
B R E A T H E   O W N U P
A   Y O   T     P
T S H I R T S   H O U S E
E   O   H   E N   E
  A U C T I O N R O O M
C   N W   O     P F
R I D G E   T R A P P E R
I   L   R O   U
S N U F F   L U M P S U M
I   F T   A E   E P
S O O T H E D   D O D G Y
```

No. 128

```
  T O L D O F F   I T C H
A   G   I R   B R   O
D E L   S H O U L D E R S
V   E   A Z A   A   T
A D D U P   E X C U S E
N   P     K O   W
C A R B O N   L A U N C H
E   E I   N     H E
  E M I N E M   D E B I T
A   A T   E B   L H
C A T H E D R A L   A W E
I   C D   I U   N R
D A H L   S T R E A K Y
```

SOLUTIONS

No. 129

```
B E F O R E · S E T O F F
R · L · E · M · Y · P · I
U S A · L O I T E R I N G
T · S · I · N · N · · H
A N K L E · U N T W I S T
L · · V · T · I · O · ·
· D O M I N E E R I N G ·
· P · · N · S · E · · A
U P T I G H T · D R E A M
R · I · · E · N · L · B
B A C K S T A G E · I L L
A · A · K · K · S · T · E
N E L L I E · A S C E N D
```

No. 130

```
B · G · D E · A · T · D
A P O L O G Y · C H O S E
N · O · W · E · T · F · L
J O D I E · S E I Z U R E
O · T · L · N · · · · T
· B U I L D I N G S I T E
S · R · · · T · · N · D
C O N S E R V A T I V E ·
U · · R · · U · E · · C
F U N F A I R · M O N T H
F · O · S · O · B · T · E
E A G L E · B E L I E V E
D · O · D E · E · D · K
```

No. 131

```
P · A · W · · R · T · B
R E F R E S H · E M A I L
O · T · R · A · L · X · E
T H E R E · I T A L I C S
E · R · R · P · S · · S
S P Y · D I S A S T E R ·
T · O · E · T · E · X · A
· S U R V E Y E D · C U B
A · · I · L · · E · A ·
S T E F A N I · S T E R N
T · M · T · S · A · D · D
O L I V E · T O R P E D O
N · T · D · · I · D · N
```

No. 132

```
A · Q · M · · L · H · T
C O U P O N · F I N I S H
I · E · R · V · C · R · O
D E S P E R A T E · E R R
I · T · O · N · · · N ·
C H I V V Y I N G · H A Y
· O · E · S · R · U · ·
T I N · R E H E A R S E D
U · · I · D · H · U · ·
R E P · M A N L I N E S S
B · A · I · G · E · D · T
A I L I N G · I N J U R E
N · M · X · · T · P · D
```

No. 133

```
T · C · S · B · W · H · B
O Z O N E · A S A R U L E
K · N · N · D · L · L · R
Y A N K I N G · L O L L Y
O · I · O · E · O · L ·
· O V E R C R O W D E D ·
· E · · · · · · · · Y ·
· A D V E R S I T I E S ·
P · · N · U · H · T · H
S O L I D · P E R G O L A
A · O · U · P · O · L ·
L I B E R A L · V I T A L
M · E · E · E · E · H · E
```

No. 134

```
A T T A C K · D E B R I S
O · W · N · O · R · N ·
E M M A · O N L O O K E R
· B · R · W · L · W · P
C O L D P L A Y · N O T E
· L · · E · M · I · · ·
H A R M E D · I C E B O X
· · A · G · X · · U · ·
E G G S · E S T I M A T E
R · S · A · U · E · R ·
N O V E M B E R · D R A M
U · U · L · E · I · G ·
S P A R S E · S H A D E D
```

No. 135

```
· P · S · D · P · K · E
· E C O N O M I S I N G ·
· L · F · O · S · T · G
P L A T E D · C L E N C H
E · N · L · E · · · U
S T E E P E N S · P I P E
· S · · · · · · · R · ·
O D D S · D E P L O Y E D
E · · I · O · D · M · ·
S T R E S S · C H U B B Y
A · A · A · K · C · R ·
· I N C O R R E C T L Y ·
· N · H · M · T · S · O
```

No. 136

```
E M E R A L D · C R U M B
O · A · O · H · A · A ·
T R A I N S P O T T I N G
A · N · E · R · · · A ·
C L O S E R U N · B U G S
· E · T · · · E · R · E
· · G O D F O R B I D · ·
T · R · U · · · C · A ·
D R U M · R E S T A R T S
A · · R · A · · B · O ·
B U R N T O F F E R I N G
· M · O · W · E · A · C
H A S T E · W R E C K E D
```

SOLUTIONS

No. 137
CROCUSES THIN
LADDER SCRUFF
DISARMED WARP
ADMISSION
GATE GYRATION
PHYSIO IMPURE
BLED FINANCES

No. 138
EDAM ATLANTIC
AVENUE ALPINE
SLUG DELAYING
WIPEOFFTHEMAP
EGGSHELL CHEW
BIKINI NAPKIN
HYDROGEN DIGS

No. 139
STAR OBSOLETE
LESSON SCRIPT
SCAR RAINDROP
DETERMINATION
LYINGLOW OURS
FEEBLE LINKED
SKILLETS EASY

No. 140
WANTED BESIDE
CONFETTI AREA
OGLE FRESHAIR
CHALLENGING
BLACKCAT YOLK
MENU GROWLING
BEAKER KICKED

No. 141
LEOTARD USUAL
GEE NAVIGATED
TULIP NEUTRAL
RHUBARB SOLAR
PENETRATE PVC
OASIS DEVIOUS

No. 142
BACKDOOR COOL
CHILLI TIMES
EDIT EXHAUSTS
SPANNING LILY
ALERT VACATE
LUNG CURLEDUP

No. 143
IMBECILE EARL
ATHENS NOUGAT
ASSAULT ADMIT
KINGS WETNESS
BASKET WARMTH
PLEA FOLLOWON

No. 144
YELLING WINCH
WING PENELOPE
SIESTA LEEK
GONG ESKIMO
SPLINTER NOAH
TOTAL FORSALE

SOLUTIONS

No. 145

```
  STOCKPILES
  H R R A L T
BRINY ENGLISH
A N P F E P E
REGATTA REPLY
E   I B     E
  MUCKRAKER
  A   I I   D
RESIT CORRODE
U C I A S R N
BLANKET TASTY
Y R K E E O
  ABANDONING
```

No. 146

```
KEEPMUM SCOUT
 S I N U O N
SCARED PASTEL
A A O S T V
SPENT STEAMER
 E H W A   N
  SAMEAGAIN
 R   I E N F
MESSAGE SHOOK
C C H U E R
COARSE SCRIMP
I A D E I A
FLUME BRITTLE
```

No. 147

```
 WROTE GRAIN
R A U   O N G
INTERN QUAVER
V H N S N A I
ELECTRICDRILL
R R H N T N L
   LENGTHY
S B T L E S P
PERMANENTWAVE
I I B T W I T
TODDLE PIGLET
E A E   S E Y
 CLASH STUDY
```

No. 148

```
 R A SAG L B
FULLUP RAISIN
 M B I E N C
MOTION ANGLER
U O N T E P
PRINTINGPRESS
E     N R   E
ASLARGEASLIFE
 C L A N I O
SHABBY DESERT
O E A S T M
HORROR ONEWAY
L T NAN N T
```

No. 149

```
  D S C F
 TRAUMATIC
N Y N N N T
VANISH CAGNEY
V N ARE E A
FIDGET RAREST
G G   G   P
BARLOW SORROW
T O RAN A O
ROTATE OWNING
R T N R G S
 THICKENED
 E H D R
```

No. 150

```
 E T R S S U
ENERGY EXTENT
R A A A O W
CARVINGS WORD
G O   H   A
REEL GREATAPE
  T R L O
HADABALL GRIM
U P   E M
ETCH HALFTIME
H U I A H U
COGNAC SIENNA
R K S H R E
```

No. 151

```
 A A M R D S
BAMBOOSHOOTS
O E N V G A
BRENDA PIGGY
T R Y
DIVORCED BOWL
V F H O A I
REEF YOUNGEST
  S B   E
MOTTO TOBAGO
O A N F O U
MANGOCHUTNEY
N E E L E S
```

No. 152

```
BEHIND SMUDGE
X C E H N U
APRESSKI LOAN
E P P R I R
ARIA ATTITUDE
I C I   I
SMOKER CANCAN
E   U A N
SNOWFALL GNAW
T O R P N
FILM EARRINGS
N A N I N E
AGENDA TOGGLE
```

No. 153

```
  H R D   A B S
CASINO   SCORCH
  R S C   W O A
OBOE   TREKKERS
  O     O L E Y
RUBBERPLANT
  R A     D L
    TROUSERSUIT
  S S   N V   O
SCOTFREE   MINK
  E O E   N O C
ONIONS   UNTRUE
  T L T   P H B
```

No. 154

```
  E H A   R S T
STEAMROLLER
  T A A   T E A
CARTON   AIDING
  T H D R     C
FEBRUARY   EVEN
      O       M
KNEW   CASHBOOK
  E L   I R   B
SAFARI   DEADLY
  R R E   I C I
  BACONANDEGG
  Y H T   G D E
```

No. 155

```
  HELPFULNESS
M V R N   E C E
ONEFORTHEROAD
U   P I D   R I
SQUEEZES   LEFT
Y P R D S C   S
  CHILL   OCEAN
L O Y   M R R P
UGLY   COLANDER
R S   L T G   I
IFTRUTHBETOLD
D E D E N   V E
  ARMOUREDCAR
```

No. 156

```
  GROUNDFROST
N U N O   I K P
OAR   BONECHINA
N A U A H   L R
DELICATE   DIES
E   K   E F F O
SADDLE   KAFTAN
C I E   U I   S
ROOT   UNPROVEN
I C T S N O   O
PREMATURE   GAS
T S L R S   U E
  TEACHERSPET
```

No. 157

```
CHAOS   MEMOIRS
A S A E   I N U
NOSEBAG   LIKED
O I R   E   D D
POSSESS   AMBLE
Y T   O G L   N
  DAMIANLEWIS
P N M G     N W
ACTUP   SHACKLE
R   U   B E   A
EASEL   ROBERTS
N I S   O O E E
TANGENT   TIDAL
```

No. 158

```
  SELFISH   STAG
P L O   U S S W
HIT   REPRODUCE
Y O C E   U N N
SINGE   RITUAL
I     H   M W
CRECHE   JEMIMA
S T E     A K
  KEEPUP   SLIME
H R A A T   C F
INNOCENCE   IOU
F A E T   R E L
IDLE   COUNTRY
```

No. 159

```
RECIPE   DISCUS
O A R S V   R P
BBC   INANYCASE
U T C   N   W N
SMILE   CURDLED
T   L T   A E
  AGRICULTURE
  L S A   P C
CLUTTER   OTHER
A T   I   I E
DETAINEES   REA
E O C S O   E T
TANKER   ONEDGE
```

No. 160

```
V O F P   M O U
INVOLVE   ELGIN
C E I G   M R C
APRON   SUBZERO
R F C   E     R
  PUSHYOURLUCK
S L   A     N S
TALCUMPOWDER
R   N     I A H
ENVELOP   LORRY
T A O   I L N E
COMMA   PROTEIN
H P D S   W D A
```

No. 161

```
A N A . . P R U
B E A R C U B . O N I O N
S . R . R . R . W . L . I
C Y C L E . O V E R E A T
E . I . . . A . R . . . E
S A S . I N D E C E N T
S . S . N . C . U . O . O
. P I E C H A R T . R U B
V . . . U . . . S . S . E
I N H A B I T . P I E R S
N . A . A . E . O . M . I
Y A C H T . R E S T A R T
L . K . E . . . Y . N . Y
```

No. 162

```
S . C D . G S . O
P O U R E D . W A S T E D
O . R . S . H . V . A . D
T E L E P H O N E . B U S
O . I . A . M . . . . . O
N E E D I N E S S . O W N
. S . R . G . K . P .
R U T . S E R V I E T T E
E . . . . . O . T . I . A
F E W . D O W N T O O L S
U . A . . . N . L . N . I
G E R A R D . D E F A C E
E . D . N . . . S . L . R
```

No. 163

```
S H . K . B . R . C . R
T R E V I . E P I S O D E
O . A . M . L . O . M . N
R A V I O L I . T E A S E
K . E . N . E . E . E . E
. U N C O N F I R M E D .
. . L . . . . . . . N . .
. T Y P E W R I T E R S .
S . . . N . E . A . O . D
C O B R A . J U B I L E E
R . A . B . E . L . L . L
A C R Y L I C . E V E N T
P . T . E . . . T . D . A
```

No. 164

```
R E D D E N . H A R A S S
S . I . I . A . U . . . W
A S K S . C A V I N G I N
E . C . O . E . . . D . R
U N B O L T E D . O N L Y
C . . . I . E . W . . . .
R E M A I N . S U N S E T
. . G . E . I . . . X . .
A S I A . P A G E A N T S
. P . I . A . N . . I . R
R E U N I T E S . M E A N
C . S . C . O . E . C . .
S K E T C H . N U D I T Y
```

No. 165

```
O F T E N . A S H A M E D
. L . M . R . M . I . L .
S O M B R E R O . S I L K
U . A . P . O . L . I . .
P R E S T O . T I E U P .
. S . S . S . H . . . S .
W A X Y . S I T . P R E Y
U . . . E . A . U . . . .
. C O A L S . L A B O U R
T . N . S . K . L . N . .
M I N D . I N E D I B L E
O . R . N . R . S . E . .
U N D E R G O . S H O T S
```

No. 166

```
G A L L E R Y . S C U B A
. C . I . O . F . A . A .
T H I G H S L A P P I N G
. I . H . I . B . . . G .
K N I T W E A R . O X E N
. G . B . . . I . S . R .
. . P U B L I C I T Y . .
S . L . O . . . R . N . .
S T U B . C O L L I D E D
A . . . K . E . C . L . .
T R E A S U R E C H E S T
. C . R . P . C . E . O .
K H A K I . C H A S I N G
```

No. 167

```
C A N D I D L Y . C A S K
. N . U . E . A . H . C .
O N E O F F . P O U T E D
U . . . E . . . B . N . .
G A R L A N D S . B A I L
. L . O . D . E . I . C .
. . N A V I G A T E S . .
B . T . N . F . S . U .
H U G H . G R A N T I N G
. B . S . R . . . R . S .
A B S O R B . E L O P E D
. L . M . A . R . I . E .
H Y P E . T U S S L I N G
```

No. 168

```
H A L F . R E C U R R E D
. L . A . E . H . E . M .
S T A T I C . E A T O U T
. E . I . A . E . R . .
D R U G . P A R T Y B A G
. A . U . . . I . . . L .
O B J E C T I O N A B L E
. L . H . . . V . . . O .
R E S C U E R S . O A T H
. . L . R . I . I . . M .
A F F I R M . N O D D E D
. E . M . A . U . E . N .
O D D B A L L S . D A T A
```

SOLUTIONS

No. 169

```
S W A N     C A U T I O U S
  H   O   O     N   N     R
F O S S I L   A W N I N G
  L   T   I     R     E
K E R R   N U M E R O U S
  S   I       E       N
F O O L H A R D I N E S S
  M   B       O   O   K
D E F R A U D S   U N I T
      E S     I   R   L
A L K A L I   E D I B L E
  O   L   V   G   S   E
S T A M P E D E   H I D E
```

No. 170

```
G L I D E R     S A L U T E
  A   R   U   A     I     E
H Y G I E N I C   M I N E
  B   E   A   H     I   S
D Y E D   W E A R T H I N
      U       A         O
  R E P L Y C O U P O N
  E           B     L
S T E A D I E S   A L S O
  R   G   T   C     S   E
G A G A   C R E A T I N G
  C   I   H     N   I   S
S T I N G Y   E X C E E D
```

No. 171

```
  A   K   P       D   S   S
F A N C L U B   A L L O T
  F   E   A   A   N   I   U
O B E   S T R O N G M A N
  R   M   L   I   L
D R A M A   E D I T I O N
  E   N   Y       N   O
D O G S H O W   W H E A T
  E   O   A   A       I
A I R W O R T H Y   O F F
  C   I   K   E   O   M   I
H I N G E   R O U T I N E
  E   G   D       T   T   D
```

No. 172

```
  C   H   G   R   P   I
N O M I N A T E   U R G E
  C   P   R   S   L   N
C O N S U L   I G L O O
  O   T   I   G       R
A N N E   C O N D O N E D
      R           C
F E A S I B L E   C A P E
  X   R   N   U   L
T A S T E   T U R R E T
  R   W   A   I   R   N
S A G O   T O R R E N T S
  S   T   H   E   D   Y
```

No. 173

```
  O   P   F   S   V   N
I M M U N I S E   I R I S
  E   N   R   E   O   C
U N L I K E   D O L L O P
  S   M           E   T
E G G H E A D   S T A I R
  O   N   P       N
B A N D Y   C L I M B E R
  L   A   U   A
H A M M E R   G A R D E N
  R   P   E   G   S   A
G E N E   A M E T H Y S T
  A   N   P   D   Y   T
```

No. 174

```
  Z   W   O       H   A
R E S O L V E   P A S T E
  B   O   E   S   L   F
A R I D   N E U R O T I C
  A   L       P       R
  G A M B L E   M U S E
  F   N   U   R   E   T
F R E D   N O B O D Y
  E       I       I   H
D I V E B O M B   T H E N
  G   D   N   I   A   N
T H I G H   W A F T I N G
  T   E       S   E   A
```

No. 175

```
  S P I D E R S W E B
    I   U   O   I   R   S
A T T I C   L E N I E N T
  C   T   H   L   C   W   Y
T R A P E Z E   E X I L E
  S   S   R       N
    R E S I S T I N G
    U       K   N       S
P O S E R   A F F L E C K
  R   H   O   T     E   L   I
O R I G A M I   R U L E D
  D   N   S   N     N   E
    G O T O G R O U N D
```